Yarn Cake
Amigurumi

Yarn Cake Amigurumi

15 cute creatures to crochet

Jacki Donhou

THE GUILD OF MASTER CRAFTSMAN PUBLICATIONS

Contents

Bunti the Bunny

Tillie the Lamb

Shawarma the Betta

Daisy the Kitten

Mischa the Otter

Weatherly the Unicorn

Romeo the Donkey

Welcome

Hello, my wonderful friends!

Even if we haven't met, our community of makers is such a close-knit bunch that we don't feel like strangers. I am bursting with joy that I get to introduce you to this collection of some of my favourite animals, all made from deliciously colourful yarn goodness.

Yarn is a uniquely visual and tactile medium. It comes in all different weights, with multiple materials – including wool, alpaca, mohair, silk, cotton, linen, acrylic and blends – to choose from. Yarn lengths vary from tiny skeins to mega balls that can take up a whole corner in my office, and come in colours that I didn't know existed.

Like many of you, I am a compulsive collector of yarn. I have a hard time resisting squishy cotton skeins and colourful hand-dyed hanks from my local shops. Recently, I have found a deep love for pre-made yarn cakes. The fun thing about yarn cakes is that I can see all the colours at once. When I envision a new design, it is exciting to map out how it could look with just one ball of cake yarn.

In this book, I wanted to combine the versatility of yarn cakes with the fun of amigurumis. Yarn cakes don't just have to be for blankets, wraps and shawls – they can make any amigurumi design look gorgeous.

I hope you love the fifteen amigurumis I have designed in this book. Happy ami making!

Jacki

Materials, tools and techniques

Materials and tools

These are the materials and tools you will need to complete the colourful projects in this book.

YARN CAKES

Yarn cakes are flat balls of yarn, wound to showcase their colour and made for easy stacking. There are thousands of premade yarn cakes available, and each brand has its collection of cakes made in different yarn weights, colours, textures, materials, lengths and other variations. This can make picking out a yarn cake for your amigurumi project fun and exciting!

When first crocheting the amigurumi in this book, take your time and select cakes that have colour variations and weights that you are comfortable with. The collection I chose for this book is Lion Brand's Mandala Ombré yarn. The seamless fade of colour hues from one colour to the next is pretty to look at, which was why I was attracted to it. Its medium, worsted-weight yarn is made of 100% acrylic, making it easy for anyone to use, no matter their skill level. But this is just my personal preference, and you should choose whatever yarn cakes you think will make an amigurumi you will treasure.

If you use a different brand or collection of yarn cakes, remember that different weight yarns will change the size and look of the final amigurumi. Lighter-weight yarn cakes will create smaller amigurumis, and because they have more length of yarn than a standard cake of the same weight, the colour changes will be over a longer length of yarn and you will have fewer colours on each of your amigurumi projects. In contrast, with heavier-weighted yarn cakes the opposite happens, so you will have larger projects with lots of colours because these yarns will have faster colour changes.

CROCHET HOOKS

Crochet hooks come in a large range of sizes. Finding the right hook size for your amigurumi project and choice of yarn can be difficult. The larger the hook, the larger your stitches will be. When working with amigurumi patterns, choosing a hook size two or three sizes smaller than what is recommended on the yarn label is ideal; this results in tighter stitches with smaller holes for the stuffing to show through. For instance, the recommended hook size for the Mandala Cake yarns is 5.5mm, but this would be for making something like a scarf, wrap or hat. Since I was making something that needed a much tighter stitch, I chose to go down to a 2.75mm hook size. This almost guarantees the stuffing will not show through the stitches.

CROCHET THREAD

Crochet thread is a very fine mercerised cotton yarn. It is not a thread used for sewing projects but is intended for delicate crochet and knitting crafts like lace work. It is mostly available in three thicknesses: size 3, size 10 and size 20, and in a range of colours. I used size 10 for my projects. It is thinner than a lightweight, fingering yarn and has the most colour options. It makes details like the outlining around the safety eyes and embroidered noses and cheeks more noticeable, which gives the amigurumis' faces more of a personality.

SAFETY EYES

Safety eyes are hard plastic eyes with washer backs. They can be found in craft supply stores. They are available in solid colours, multi-colours and even glitter for added sparkle. I have used ½in (12mm) solid black eyes for all of my patterns. See page 23 for instructions on how to attach them. Please note that if you are making an amigurumi for a young child, it is advisable to embroider the eyes on rather than using safety eyes. Safety eyes are small and can be dangerous if removed by a small child.

STUFFING

Polyester fibre filling is a synthetic hypoallergenic fibre made for pillows, crafts and toys. When you stuff an amigurumi piece, you want it to be firm enough to hold its shape but not over-stuffed. Follow the steps clearly, as some pieces include instructions on how to stuff.

EMBROIDERY NEEDLES

Embroidery needles are long needles with a large eye used to sew together and attach the amigurumi pieces. With my patterns, I tend to use two needles: a larger needle with a blunt tip to sew the body parts together approximately 7in (17.5cm) in total length with an eye 1in (2.5cm) long, and a smaller needle with a sharp tip approximately 1½in (4cm) in total length for the eye details. If you find another size needle that works best for you, use the more comfortable size.

SCISSORS

Using a small pair of embroidery scissors with sharp tips is best. When you need to trim yarn ends after finishing off, smaller scissors lessen the risk of cutting through and damaging the other stitches.

SEWING PINS

Use these stick pins to keep all your amigurumi body parts secured and in place for sewing. Pins with a ball or a heart on the top are easier to use and give you something to hold.

They are also easier to see against the crocheted surface. Pins with a flat top are not recommended, because they can get lost in your amigurumi pieces. I like to use a lot of pins, so my pieces stay in the correct place and do not move while I am attaching them. Pins will also be needed for mapping out the clustered spots on Garrick the Dragon's body.

STITCH MARKERS

Stitch markers are plastic or metal clasps that hook onto your crochet work and are designed to keep track of either the starting or the ending stitch in your rounds. As you crochet from round 1 and on, you can move your stitch marker up to the next round.

PET BRUSH

A coarse brush with wire or firm nylon bristles is used to brush out yarn and make hair-like strands or give a fur-like texture to the amigurumi pieces. For example, the pompom tail on Bunti the Bunny (page 33) is brushed out at the end to make it fluffy.

POMPOMS

A pompom is a small decorative ball of fur or yarn. These are available in different colours and sizes or can easily be made by wrapping yarn around your hand or buying a pompom maker. A pompom is needed for Bunti the Bunny's tail. Full instructions for making a pompom are given in that project (see page 33), or you can buy a readymade one.

Stitches and techniques

Here we explain the crochet stitches and techniques you will need to be familiar with in order to make the projects in this book. With easy-to-follow instructions and clear illustrations, you'll be making the cutest yarn cake amigurumi in no time.

HOLDING A HOOK

To hold a crochet hook, use your dominant hand to grip the hook and your less dominant hand for holding the yarn.

Hold the crochet hook at a downward angle, like a knife.

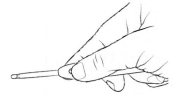

HOLDING YARN

There are many ways to hold the yarn while you crochet. It all depends on which hold is the most comfortable for you to maintain the right amount of tension.

If the yarn tension is too tight as you crochet, inserting the crochet hook in the next set of stitches could be difficult. If the tension is too loose, you will create holes in the rounds through which the stuffing could show. Take the time to find a hold that suits you.

Step 1: A simple way to hold the yarn is to begin by wrapping it around your little finger, then carry it under the next two fingers and over the index finger.

Step 2: Your thumb and middle finger will then grip the tail end of the yarn to hold it in place. Elevate your index finger to add the tension the yarn needs and make your first stitch.

MAKING A SLIPKNOT

Almost all pieces of crochet will begin with a slipknot.

Holding the yarn end, make a loop by crossing the yarn over itself. Insert the hook through the centre of the loop, yarn over the hook and pull the hook back through the centre. Pull the yarn end to tighten the loop on the hook to create the slipknot.

CHAIN STITCH (ch)

A chain stitch is a basic stitch that is mostly used to start or end a row.

Step 1: Starting with a slipknot, wrap the yarn around the crochet hook.

Step 2: Simply pull the yarn through the loop on the hook to form the first chain.

Step 3: If you need to make several chains, repeat the steps until you have the required number of chains.

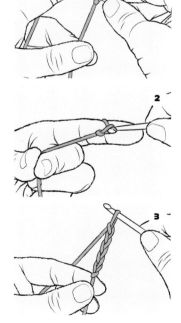

SLIP STITCH (sl st)

The slip stitch has more than one use in a pattern, adding a detailed seam to a piece and sometimes connecting pieces together.

Step 1: Insert the crochet hook under the stitch and wrap the yarn around the crochet hook.

Step 2: Pull the yarn through the stitch and through the loop on the crochet hook. If needing to make several slip stitches, repeat the steps until you have the number of slip stitches for the pattern.

DOUBLE CROCHET (dc)

Double crochet is the main stitch used for the projects.

Step 1: Insert the crochet hook under both loops of the stitch or the chain space.

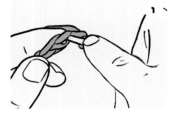

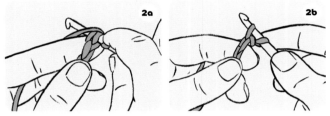

Step 2: Wrap the yarn around the crochet hook and pull the yarn through the stitch. There will be two loops on the crochet hook.

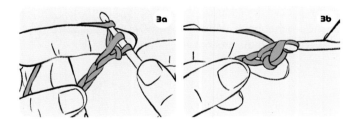

Step 3: Wrap the yarn around the crochet hook once more and pull the yarn through both loops on the crochet hook.

TREBLE (tr)

Treble stitch is a taller version of double crochet.

Step 1: Wrap the yarn around the crochet hook and then insert the hook under the stitch or the chain space.

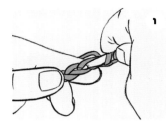

Step 2: Wrap the yarn around the crochet hook and pull the yarn through the stitch. There will be three loops on the crochet hook. Wrap the yarn around the crochet hook again.

Step 3: Pull the yarn through two of the loops on the crochet hook, leaving two loops on the crochet hook. Then, wrap the yarn around the hook once more.

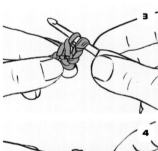

Step 4: Pull the yarn through the last two remaining loops on the crochet hook.

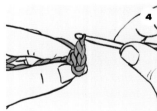

3rd LOOP

The 3rd loop of a double crochet stitch is on the back side of the row and below the back loop. It runs horizontally like a line or bar behind the stitch. Grab this loop with the point of the hook rather than pushing the hook under the loop. It makes it easier in case the tension is tighter. You will see this used to make the ribbing for Shawarma the Betta's tail (see page 66).

DOUBLE TREBLE (dtr)

Double treble stitch is an even taller stitch that starts by wrapping the yarn around the crochet hook two times at the beginning of the stitch.

Step 1: Wrap the yarn around the crochet hook twice and then insert the hook under the stitch or the chain space.

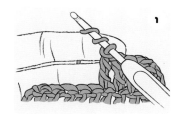

Step 2: Wrap the yarn around the crochet hook and pull the yarn through the stitch. There will be four loops on the crochet hook.

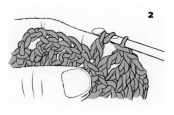

Step 3: Wrap the yarn around the crochet hook again and pull the yarn through two of the four loops on the crochet hook. This will leave three loops on the crochet hook. Wrap the yarn around the crochet hook and pull the yarn through two of the three loops on the crochet hook, leaving two loops on the crochet hook.

Step 4: Wrap the yarn around the crochet hook once more and pull the yarn through the last two loops on the crochet hook to complete the stitch.

HALF TREBLE (htr)

Half treble stitch is similar to the double crochet but starts by wrapping the yarn around the crochet hook at the beginning of the stitch.

Step 1: Wrap the yarn around the crochet hook, then insert the hook under the stitch or the chain space.

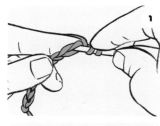

Step 2: Wrap the yarn around the crochet hook and pull the yarn through the stitch. There will be three loops on the crochet hook.

Step 3: Wrap the yarn around the crochet hook once more and pull the yarn through all three loops on the crochet hook.

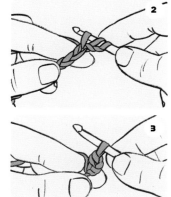

WORK 2 HALF TREBLE STITCHES INTO THE NEXT STITCH TO INCREASE (htr2inc)

Another way to increase a row or a round is to use two half treble stitches.

Work two of the same stitches in the same stitch or chain space. This will increase the stitch count by one stitch.

WORK 2 DOUBLE CROCHET STITCHES TOGETHER TO DECREASE (dc2tog)

A decrease is to crochet two stitches together to shorten a row or round. The method shown here is for an invisible decrease, where the front loops of the two stitches are pulled together so that the back loops collapse behind the stitch to close up the small hole and prevent the stuffing from showing.

Step 1: Insert the hook under the front loop only of the stitch. Then, insert the hook under the front loop only of the next stitch.

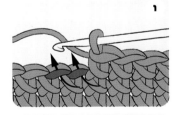

WORK 2 DOUBLE CROCHET STITCHES INTO THE NEXT STITCH TO INCREASE (dc2inc)

Working two stitches in the same space is a way to make a row or round larger (known as increasing).

Work two of the same stitches in the same stitch or chain space. This will increase the stitch count by one stitch.

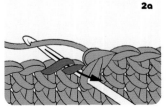
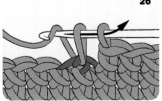

Step 2: With three loops on the hook, yarn over and pull through both the front loops. This leaves two loops left on the hook. Yarn over and pull through the last two loops.

MAGIC CIRCLE (mc)

The magic circle or ring is the cleanest way to begin a round when crocheting, especially when making amigurumi. It is an adjustable ring with an end, usually made with double crochet stitches, that tightens to close the centre of the first round.

Step 1: Holding the yarn end, make a loop by crossing the yarn over itself. Then, grip that crossing point, insert the hook through the centre of the loop, wrap the yarn around the crochet hook, and pull the hook back through the centre.

Step 2: While still holding the circle, wrap the yarn around the crochet hook and pull the yarn through the loop on the hook to form the first chain. This step is worked around the circle.

Step 3: Insert the crochet hook through the circle, wrap the yarn around the hook and pull the yarn through. There will be two loops on the crochet hook.

Step 4: Wrap the yarn around the crochet hook once more and pull the yarn through both loops on the crochet hook.

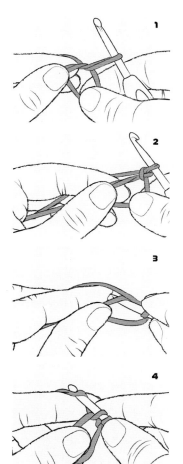

Step 5: This completes the first double crochet stitch on the magic circle. Repeat the steps until you have the number of double crochet stitches for the pattern.

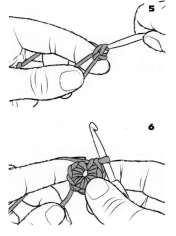

Step 6: Gently pull the yarn end to tighten and close the magic circle. When working the horns on Weatherly the Unicorn and Garrick the Dragon, you will need to leave the magic circle open so you can stuff them.

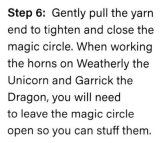

BACK LOOP ONLY (BLO)

The top of a stitch has two loops, a front loop and a back loop. The back loop is the loop that is the furthest from you and the only loop the crochet hook will work under, leaving the closest loop, the front loop, unworked. When working in the back loop only, it changes the effect of the piece you are working on. It reshapes your work and forces the stitches back from their original position. This happens when moving from a paw to a leg on the amigurumi. It also leaves the front loop visible so you can come back to it later and add a detail or edging, such as Garrick the Dragon's horns (see page 128).

Insert the hook under the loop of the next stitch that is furthest away, not under both loops of the next stitch.

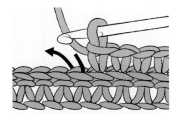

BOBBLE STITCH (BOB)

Bobble stitches are little puffy balls crocheted into the pattern to add toes and thumbs. They are made from six unfinished treble crochet left on the hook within the same stitch and then closed at the end. This stitch is used for Garrick the Dragon's feet and Mischa the Otter's arms.

Step 1: Yarn over and insert the hook under the next stitch. Yarn over and pull through the stitch, yarn over again and pull through two stitches. Repeat these steps five times until there are six loops on the hook.

Step 2: Yarn over and pull through all six loops.

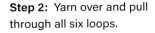
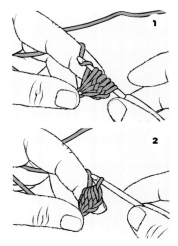

FRONT LOOP ONLY (FLO)

The front loop of the stitch is the loop that is closest to you and the only loop the crochet hook will work under, leaving the BLO unworked. When working FLO stitches, it changes the positioning of the stitches and curves your next rounds or rows forward. This will happen when making the feet of Biscuit the Duck (see page 36), curving the structure of the feet to create an ankle after working in the FLO. This technique is also used when closing up a head made from bottom to top by tightening up the last round.

Insert the hook under the loop of the next stitch that is nearest you, not under both loops of the next stitch.

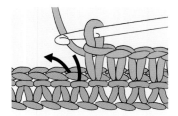

POPCORN STITCH (POP)

Popcorn stitches are small oval-shaped puffy stitches crocheted into the pattern to add details like wool fleece. They are made from five treble crochet in the same stitch and then closed at the top to make them stand out. This is used to make Tillie the Lamb's curly fleece, Neville the Alpaca's hooves and Jasper the Puppy's paws.

Step 1: Start by making five treble crochet in the designated stitch.

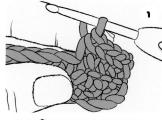

Step 2: Carefully remove the hook from the last loop, leaving it intact for later, and insert the hook back under the top stitch of the first treble.

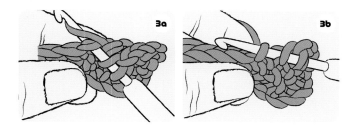

Step 3: Grab the last loop with the hook and pull through the stitch.

LOOP STITCH (LP)

The loop stitch is a more advanced crochet stitch and takes some practice to get it right. The loops are created by wrapping the yarn around your finger before completing. This stitch is used to make Neville the Alpaca's curly mane (see page 120).

Step 1: Insert the hook under the next stitch. Wrap the yarn around your index finger, then yarn over to push the yarn on the hook to the left.

Step 2: Hook the strand wrapped behind the index finger.

Step 3: Pull through at the stitch. There should be only two loops on the hook. Yarn over and finish the stitch as usual.

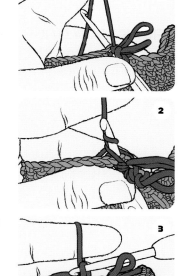

CHANGING COLOURS

When working on a pattern using yarn cakes, this is a fun way to showcase the dye technique and the colour flows of each one. Even though many of the patterns are worked bottom to top or vice versa, showcasing the yarn cake's colour transitions, there are instances where colour changes are needed. Hazel the Cow has spots that stand out visually, so a colour change within the specific rounds is necessary.

Step 1: When you need to change a colour in a round, leave the last stitch of the previous colour unfinished without pulling the final loop through the stitch.

Step 2: Wrap the new colour around the hook and pull through the leftover loops.

Step 3: Continue the new colour in the next stitch or stitches. Tie the loose tails in a knot and leave them inside the crocheted piece.

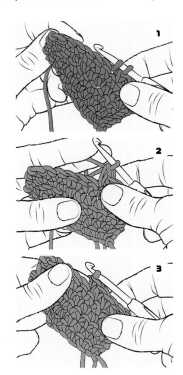

YARN OVER AND YARN UNDER

When discussing how to make your stitches with either yarn over or yarn under, remember there is never a right way or a wrong way; it just comes down to what you are more comfortable with.

Yarn over happens when you hook the yarn strand from underneath, forcing the yarn on top of the hook. When pulled through the stitch to make a double crochet, the result looks like a V-shape.

Yarn under happens when you hook the top of the yarn strand, wrapping it under the hook. When pulled through the stitch to make a double crochet, the result looks like an X-shape.

Working with yarn under, the stitches come out tighter, with fewer holes between them, resulting in a small amigurumi. The yarn over technique has the opposite effect: the stitches will come out slightly large, which in turn makes the resulting amigurumi pieces bigger.

INVISIBLE FASTEN OFF IN A ROUND

Fastening off in a round can leave a noticeable bump. So, choosing to do an invisible fasten-off will leave the stitches having a cleaner finish to the round.

Step 1: Cut the end of the yarn leaving a yarn tail of about 4in (10cm). Pull the loop up and out of the last stitch.

Step 2: With a large embroidery needle, thread the tail through the eye of the needle. Before moving on, count the stitches in the round backwards and mark the first stitch of that round. Insert the needle under both of the top loops of the second stitch that is next to the marked stitch. This will overlap the first stitch, ensuring that we keep the same number of stitches in the round.

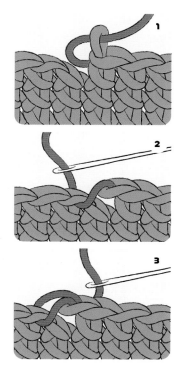

Step 3: Pull the needle up and insert it underneath the back loop of the last stitch in the round. This is the same stitch the yarn started from. Weave in the tail on the back or inside of the piece.

FASTEN OFF IN A ROW

Fastening off at the end of a row is very important. Leaving the tail end of the yarn exposed or loose can result in the piece unravelling and you losing all your hard work. Properly fastening off can prevent that from happening.

Cut the end of the yarn leaving a yarn tail of about 4in (10cm). Pull the tail up through the loop with the hook.

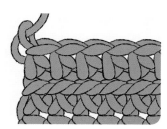

WEAVING IN THE ENDS AFTER SEWING

Weaving in the loose ends is usually the final step in any crochet project. All the leftover yarn from sewing can sometimes seem like a lot of work. To not get overwhelmed, it is best to weave in a few of the ends as you sew the pieces together.

Step 1: Thread a large embroidery needle with the end or yarn tail, then insert the needle through the amigurumi piece and out at a location that is inconspicuous. Insert the needle underneath a few stitches along one of the rows or rounds.

Step 2: Pull the yarn slightly tight and then reverse to come back in the other direction under a few more stitches. Hide the remaining yarn tail in the amigurumi piece.

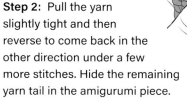

Finishing touches

This next section will teach you the how-to's of sewing all the pieces together and adding those special details to your amigurumi. It is the last step of completing your amigurumi so you can sit back and enjoy your accomplishments.

WHIP STITCH

Whip stitch is used to attach the body parts together.

First make sure the two pieces are pinned against each other in the location the pattern states. Thread the large embroidery needle with the leftover tail of the first piece being attached and insert the needle under the stitch of the matched-up 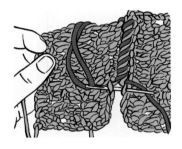 stitch on the second piece and pull it through. Next, bring the needle back up and under both loops of the next stitch on the piece that is being attached and pull it tight. Then insert the needle under the next stitch of the second piece. Repeat the steps until both pieces are secure.

To add whip stitches to noses or cheeks using the small embroidery needle (for example, to add detail to the cheeks on Emilio the Axolotl, page 86), insert the needle in the first location stated in the instructions and out at the second location. Repeat the steps until the number of whip stitches needed have been completed.

MATTRESS STITCH

This stitch is used to attach Tillie the Lamb's hair cap (see page 60) and Weatherly the Unicorn's hair (see page 107).

Step 1: First make sure the two pieces are pinned against each other in the location the pattern states. Thread a large embroidery needle with the leftover tail of the first piece, insert the needle under the stitch post or bar of the matched-up stitch on the second piece and pull it through tightly. The stitch post or bar is the yarn in between each round that connects the two.

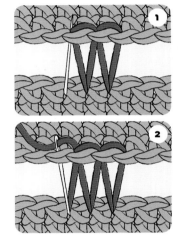

Step 2: Insert the needle back through the same hole you started on the first piece and out under the next stitch post, then pull it though. Repeat the steps until both pieces are secure.

LOOP AND HOOK FOR ADDING HAIR

Full instructions are given in the steps for Aggie the Highland Bull (see page 54) and Romeo the Donkey (see page 114).

Step 1: Fold the piece of trimmed yarn in half. Insert the crochet hook under the stitch in the round indicated in the pattern. Grab the centre of the folded piece of yarn with the crochet hook and pull it partway through the stitch, making a loop.

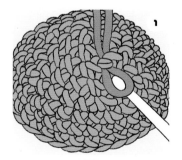

Step 2: With the crochet hook still in the loop, grab the end section of the yarn and draw it through the loop and tighten.

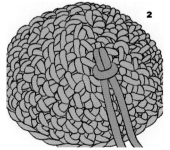

ADDING SAFETY EYES

Note that safety eyes are small and can be dangerous if removed by a small child.

Place the stem of the black safety eye through the skipped stitch on the round indicated in the pattern. With the stem exposed on the inside of the crocheted head, firmly push the washer over the stem until it clicks into place. The tighter the washer is against the back side of the safety eye, the less chance your eye details will slip under them. If you are working with washers that are curved or a cup shape, make sure the open cup side of the washer is placed on the stem first. This will sink the eye into the washer and help to prevent it from falling off.

OUTLINING THE SAFETY EYES

Safety eyes on amigurumi are usually solid black and very dull. When crochet thread is used to outline each of the eyes, it gives the amigurumi a realistic featured face, adding a sweet expression to each of them.

Step 1: Using white crochet thread, push the needle through the bottom of the head and out at the inside bottom corner of the first eye (I tend to use a smaller embroidery needle with a sharp tip for this). Then insert your needle back through the top outside  corner of the eye (diagonal corner of the eye). Pull the thread through the head and out the same stitch or near where you entered. This adds a stripe to the lower portion of the eye. Do not pull too tight otherwise the thread may slip under the eye.

Step 2: Secure this thread in place by having it come back up and circle the middle of the thread strand. Take the needle back through the bottom of the head at the starting point, tie it off and hide the thread tail inside the head. Then repeat the steps for the second eye.

Step 3: Starting with black crochet thread, push the needle through the bottom of the head and out, at the inside bottom corner of the first eye. Insert your needle back through the top outside corner of the eye (diagonal corner of the eye), but a stitch away from the  white thread. Pull the thread through the head and out the same stitch or near where you entered. Do not pull too tight otherwise the thread may slip under the eye.

Step 4: Secure this thread in place by having it come back up and circle the middle of the thread strand. Take the needle back through the bottom of the head at the starting point, tie it off and hide the thread tail inside the head. Then repeat the steps for the second eye.

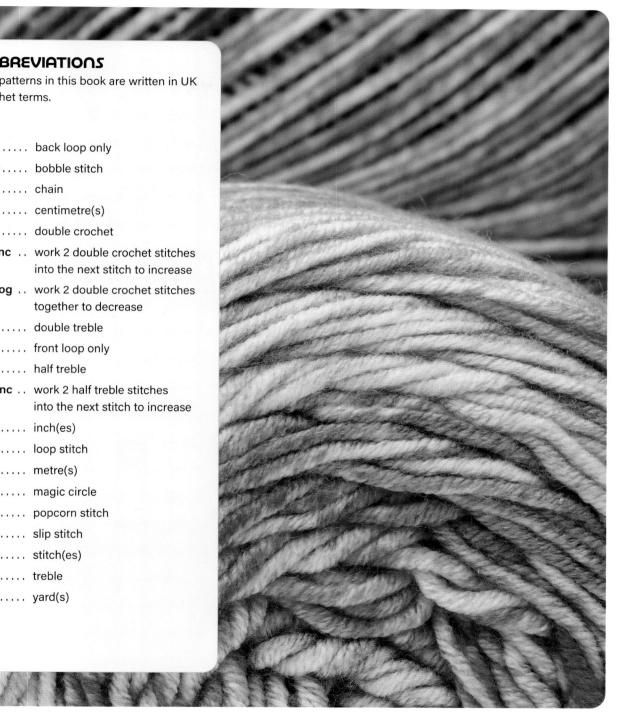

ABBREVIATIONS

The patterns in this book are written in UK crochet terms.

BLO . . . . . back loop only

BOB . . . . . bobble stitch

ch . . . . chain

cm . . . . . . centimetre(s)

dc . . . . double crochet

dc2inc . . work 2 double crochet stitches into the next stitch to increase

dc2tog . . work 2 double crochet stitches together to decrease

dtr . . . . . . double treble

FLO . . . . . front loop only

htr . . . . . . half treble

htr2inc . . work 2 half treble stitches into the next stitch to increase

in . . . . inch(es)

LP . . . . . . loop stitch

m . . . . metre(s)

MC . . . . . . magic circle

POP . . . . . popcorn stitch

sl st . . . . . slip stitch

st(s) . . . . . stitch(es)

tr . . . . treble

yd . . . . yard(s)

The
Designs

Bunti the Bunny

Bunti is the youngest of fourteen brothers and sisters (but that will change very soon). She likes fresh clover from the pasture, drinking from the cool brook and watching that silly puppy trying to herd sheep. How can a puppy that small think he could possibly make a sheep listen to him? Still, maybe one day he will. Bunti will tell everyone when it finally happens!

Skill Level

Finished size

8in (20cm)

Supplies and materials

Lion Brand Mandala Ombré, 100% acrylic (344yd/315m per 150g)

1 ball in Serene

Size 10 crochet thread in black, white and pink

2.75mm (US C/2) crochet hook

2 x ½in (12mm) safety eyes

Polyester fibre filling

Large and small embroidery needles

Scissors

Sewing pins

1½in (4cm) readymade pompom, or use the yarn cake to make your own (see instructions on page 33)

Pet brush

Work the yarn cake from start to finish in a continuous motion. We will not be cutting the yarn and choosing colours. Working in this fashion, the colour changes in the yarn cake will work up the bunny from the feet to the ears.

Starting with either the inside or the outside of the cake, work all the stitches in a round. Then, when instructed, work in rows.

FEET (MAKE 2)

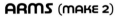

Work all the stitches in a round.
Stuff as you crochet up to round 13.
Round 1: Make a MC with 6 dc (6 sts).
Round 2: (Dc2inc) 6 times (12 sts).
Round 3: (Dc, dc2inc) 6 times (18 sts).
Round 4: *5 dc, (dc2inc) 4 times; rep from * to end of round (26 sts).
Rounds 5–7: Dc in each st around.
Round 8: 6 dc, (dc2tog) 4 times, 12 dc (22 sts).
Round 9: 5 dc, (dc2tog) 3 times, 11 dc (19 sts).
Round 10: Dc in each st around.
Round 11: (Dc2tog) 7 times, 5 dc (12 sts).
Rounds 12–17: Dc in each st around.
Pinch the leg closed. If your seam is not centred with the decreases on the feet, add or subtract 1–3 stitches.
Dc through both sides with 6 dc and close the opening (6 sts).
Fasten off and leave a long tail for attaching.

BODY

Continuing the current cake yarn colour, work all the stitches in a round.
Stuff as you crochet.
Round 1: Make a MC with 6 dc (6 sts).

Round 2: (Dc2inc) 6 times (12 sts).
Round 3: (Dc, dc2inc) 6 times (18 sts).
Round 4: (Dc, dc2inc, dc) 6 times (24 sts).
Round 5: (3 dc, dc2inc) 6 times (30 sts).
Round 6: (2 dc, dc2inc, 2 dc) 6 times (36 sts).
Rounds 7–12: Dc in each st around.
Round 13: (2 dc, dc2tog, 2 dc) 6 times (30 sts).
Rounds 14–16: Dc in each st around.
Round 17: (3 dc, dc2tog) 6 times (24 sts).
Rounds 18–19: Dc in each st around.
Round 20: (Dc, dc2tog, dc) 6 times (18 sts).
Rounds 21–22: Dc in each st around.
Round 23: (Dc, dc2tog) 6 times (12 sts).
Fasten off, leaving a long tail for attaching.

ARMS (MAKE 2)

Continuing the current cake yarn colour, work all the stitches in a round.
Stuff as you crochet up to round 11.
Round 1: Make a MC with 6 dc (6 sts).

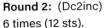

Round 2: (Dc2inc) 6 times (12 sts).
Round 3: (Dc, dc2inc) 6 times (18 sts).
Round 4: Dc in each st around.
Round 5: 3 dc, (dc2tog) 6 times, 3 dc (12 sts).
Rounds 6–17: Dc in each st around.
Pinch the arm closed. If your seam is not centred with the decreases on the arms, add or subtract 1–3 stitches.
Dc through both sides with 6 dc and close the opening (6 sts).
Fasten off, leaving a long tail for attaching.

HEAD

Continuing the current cake yarn colour, work all the stitches in a round from bottom to top.
Stuff as you crochet.

Round 1: Make a MC with 6 dc (6 sts).
Round 2: (Dc2inc) 6 times (12 sts).
Round 3: (Dc, dc2inc) 6 times (18 sts).
Round 4: (Dc, dc2inc, dc) 6 times (24 sts).
Round 5: (3 dc, dc2inc) 6 times (30 sts).
Round 6: (2 dc, dc2inc, 2 dc) 6 times (36 sts).
Round 7: (5 dc, dc2inc) 6 times (42 sts).
Rounds 8–11: Dc in each st around.
Round 12: (5 dc, dc2tog) 6 times (36 sts).
Round 13: 12 dc, 1 ch, skip 1 dc, 10 dc, 1 ch, skip 1 dc, 12 dc (36 sts).
Note: the chain spaces in round 13 are where you place the safety eyes later.
Rounds 14–19: Dc in each st around.
Add the safety eyes in the chain spaces on round 13.
Round 20: (2 dc, dc2tog, 2 dc) 6 times (30 sts).
Round 21: Dc in each st around.
Round 22: (3 dc, dc2tog) 6 times (24 sts).
Round 23: (Dc, dc2tog, dc) 6 times (18 sts).
Round 24: (Dc, dc2tog) 6 times (12 sts).
Round 25: (Dc, dc2tog) 4 times (8 sts).
Fasten off and weave the yarn under each of the FLO, pull tight and hide the end inside the head.

. . . .

EARS (MAKE 2)

Continuing the current cake yarn colour, work all the stitches in a row from bottom to top.
When crocheting in a chain, after turning, htr in the first htr from the hook. Chains do not count as stitches.

Row 1: Ch 3, 3 htr in 3rd ch from hook, ch 2, turn (3 sts).
Row 2: Htr2inc, 1 htr, htr2inc, ch 2, turn (5 sts).
Row 3: Htr2inc, 3 htr, htr2inc, ch 2, turn (7 sts).

Row 4: Htr2inc, 5 htr, htr2inc, ch 2, turn (9 sts).
Row 5: Htr2inc, 7 htr, htr2inc, ch 2, turn (11 sts).
Row 6: Htr2inc, 9 htr, htr2inc, ch 2, turn (13 sts).
Row 7: Htr2inc, 11 htr, htr2inc, ch 2, turn (15 sts).
Rows 8–12: Htr in each st across, ch 2, turn.
Round 13: Dc around the ear (including along row 12), making sure to put 3 dc at the top of the ear.
Fold the bottom of the ear in half away from the forward-facing edging from round 13. Then, fold the ends of the bottom of the ear forward towards the middle of the first fold. Dc through all 4 folded rows on the bottom of the ear with 5 dc and close the opening (5 sts).
Fasten off and leave a long tail for attaching.

MAKING UP

EYES

Outline the safety eyes inserted on round 13 of the head using the small embroidery needle and white and black crochet thread (see page 24).

NOSE

Make an upside-down triangle nose using the small embroidery needle and the pink crochet thread. Insert sewing pins to outline the nose beginning 1 round down from the safety eyes, 4 stitches wide, 2 rounds long, with 2 stitches between each safety eye and the pin. Pull your thread through the bottom of the head and out the top corner pin. Then, embroider a triangle from the top corner to the lower pin. Continue moving your thread along the same round where the top corner pins are located and through the same bottom pin hole in a fan-like shape. Once finished, outline the top of the upside-down triangle with 3 whip stitches. Bring the needle back down through the head to where it entered. Tie the thread ends together and hide them within the head.

EARS

Pin the ears to the top of the head starting at the last round. The cup shape of the ears needs to be facing the front of the head. Pin the back of the ears towards the side of the head at round 22. This will leave 4 stitches on round 22 between the ears on the back of the head. Once the placement is correct, sew the ears in place using whip stitches with the large embroidery needle. Weave in the end when finished.

HEAD AND BODY

Before attaching the head to the body, use pins to ensure the placement is correct. You want the head to be slightly forward to create the look of a larger chin. Once aligned, attach the head and body by using the large embroidery needle and the long tail left over from the body to whip stitch the two together. Weave in the end when finished.

FEET AND ARMS

Pin the feet between rounds 5–6 to 9–10 and angled forward so the heels touch the surface they are on. Make sure the bunny can sit on its own before sewing. If not, adjust the feet up or down 1 or 2 rounds to get a perfect sitting position.

Once even, whip stitch the feet to the sides of the body using the large embroidery needle. Add a few whip stitches along the bottom back of the leg portion of the feet to ensure they are secured and don't move around. When complete, secure and weave in the end.

The arms should be pinned 1 round down from the head between rounds 22 and 23 and on the sides of the body, leaving at least 5 stitches between them on the back at the tops of the arms. Angle the arms slightly forward and down so the arms are touching the legs. If they are even, you can whip stitch the pieces to the body with the large embroidery needle. If not, adjust the arms up or down to ensure a good placement. When complete, secure and weave in the end.

TAIL

If you're making your own pompom, continue the yarn on the cake. Cut a piece of yarn 7in (17.5cm) and set it aside. Wrap the continuing yarn colour from the cake around your hand 75 times. Take the long piece of cut yarn and tie a knot around the yarn bundle. Remove it from your hands and lay it on the centre of the cut yarn. Flip it over, add a second knot in the back, and cut through both loops. Shake gently and use your scissors to shape the pompom, cutting any longer yarn ends. Hold the pompom firmly and lightly brush the yarn ends with a pet brush to create a fluffy, full pompom. Using the large embroidery needle, whip stitch the pompom onto the lower back at round 9.

Biscuit the Duck

Biscuit likes to spend his days hanging out at the big pond watching his older brothers and sisters swim and play. He's still too small to go out on his own, but he's happy to swim alongside his mother and dream of the day he can chase the dragonflies in the afternoon sun. Until then, he just has to keep practising his quacks.

Skill Level

Finished size

5in (12.5cm)

Supplies and materials

Lion Brand Mandala Ombré, 100% acrylic (344yd/315m per 150g)

1 ball in Tranquil

Size 10 crochet threads in black and white

2.75mm (US C/2) crochet hook

2 x ½in (12mm) safety eyes

Polyester fibre filling

Large and small embroidery needles

Scissors

Sewing pins

Stitch markers

The duck will be made by choosing the three colours from either the yarn cake's centre pull or the three colours from the outside starting pull. The first colour will be used for the beak and feet, the second for the body and wings, and the third for the head.

Each colour will be used, then the extra cut and set aside. Starting with either the inside or the outside of the cake, work all the stitches in a round, unless otherwise instructed.

FEET (MAKE 2)

When crocheting in a chain, after turning, dc in the 2nd chain from the hook.
Do not stuff.
Row 1: Ch 7, turn (7 sts).
Round 1: 5 dc, 3 dc in end ch, 5 dc in reverse side of chain, 3 dc in end ch (16 sts).

Round 2: 6 dc, dc2inc, 7 dc, dc2inc, dc (18 sts).
Rounds 3–5: Dc in each st around.
Round 6: 2 dc, dc2tog, 7 dc, dc2tog, 5 dc (16 sts).
Round 7: (Dc2tog, dc, dc2tog, 3 dc) twice (12 sts).
Round 8: (Dc, dc2tog) 4 times (8 sts).
Rounds 9–10: 3 dc, 5 htr.
Round 11: Dc in each st around.
Fasten off and leave a long tail for attaching.

BEAK

Continuing the first colour, work all the stitches in a round.
Do not stuff.
Round 1: Make a MC with 5 dc (5 sts).
Round 2: Dc in each st around.
Round 3: (Dc2inc) 5 times (10 sts).
Round 4: Dc in each st around.
Round 5: (Dc, dc2inc) 5 times (15 sts).
Pinch the beak closed, dc through both sides with 7 dc, and close the opening (7 sts).
Fasten off and leave a long tail for attaching.

This will be the end of the first colour. Cut any yarn left on the cake that needs to be trimmed off and set aside. You will continue the next part with the second colour.

BODY

With the next cake yarn colour, work all the stitches in a round from bottom to top.
Stuff as you crochet.
Round 1: Make a MC with 6 dc (6 sts).
Round 2: (Dc2inc) 6 times (12 sts).
Round 3: (Dc, dc2inc) 6 times (18 sts).
Round 4: (Dc, dc2inc, dc) 6 times (24 sts).
Round 5: (3 dc, dc2inc) 6 times (30 sts).
Round 6: (2 dc, dc2inc, 2 dc) 6 times (36 sts).

Round 7: (5 dc, dc2inc) 6 times (42 sts).
Round 8: 36 dc, (dc2inc) in the next 5 sts, dc (47 sts).
Rounds 9–10: Dc in each st around.
Round 11: 40 dc, dc2tog, 5 dc (46 sts).
Round 12: 38 dc, dc2tog, dc, dc2tog, 3 dc (44 sts).
Round 13: 36 dc, (dc2tog) in the next 4 sts (40 sts).
Round 14: (4 dc, dc2tog, 4 dc) 4 times (36 sts).
Rounds 15–18: Dc in each st around.
Round 19: (2 dc, dc2tog, 2 dc) 6 times (30 sts).
Rounds 20–22: Dc in each st around.
Round 23: (3 dc, dc2tog) 6 times (24 sts).
Round 24: Dc in each st around.
Round 25: (1 dc, dc2tog, 1 dc) 6 times (18 sts).
Fasten off and leave a long tail for attaching.

WINGS (MAKE 2)

Continuing the current cake yarn colour, work all the stitches in a round. Do not stuff.
Round 1: Make a MC with 6 dc (6 sts).
Round 2: Dc in each st around.
Round 3: (Dc2inc) 6 times (12 sts).
Rounds 4–5: Dc in each st around.
Round 6: (Dc, dc2inc) 6 times (18 sts).
Rounds 7–9: Dc in each st around.
Round 10: (Dc, dc2tog) 6 times (12 sts).
Round 11: Dc in each st around.
Round 12: 2 dc, (dc2tog) in the next 4 sts, 2 dc (8 sts).
Pinch the wing closed, dc through both sides with 4 dc, and close the opening (4 sts).
Fasten off and leave a long tail for attaching.

This will be the end of the second colour. Cut any yarn left on the cake that needs to be trimmed off and set aside. You will continue the next part with the third colour.

If the second colour was shorter than expected, and the third colour has already been worked into the pattern, just keep crocheting.

HEAD

With the next cake yarn colour, work all the stitches in a round from bottom to top.
Stuff as you crochet.
Round 1: Make a MC with 6 dc (6 sts).
Round 2: (Dc2inc) 6 times (12 sts).
Round 3: (Dc, dc2inc) 6 times (18 sts).
Round 4: (Dc, dc2inc, dc) 6 times (24 sts).
Round 5: (3 dc, dc2inc) 6 times (30 sts).
Round 6: (2 dc, dc2inc, 2 dc) 6 times (36 sts).
Round 7: (5 dc, dc2inc) 6 times (42 sts).
Rounds 8–10: Dc in each st around.
Round 11: 10 dc, (dc2inc) twice, 18 dc, (dc2inc) twice, 10 dc (46 sts).
Round 12: Dc in each st around.
Round 13: 10 dc, (dc2tog) twice, 3 dc, 1 ch, skip 1 dc, 10 dc, 1 ch, skip 1 dc, 3 dc, (dc2tog) twice, 10 dc (42 sts).
Note: the chain spaces in round 13 are where you place the safety eyes later.
Round 14: 10 dc, dc2tog, 18 dc, dc2tog, 10 dc (40 sts).
Rounds 15–17: Dc in each st around.
Add the safety eyes in the chain spaces on round 13.
Round 18: (4 dc, dc2tog, 4 dc) 4 times (36 sts).
Rounds 19–20: Dc in each st around.
Round 21: (2 dc, dc2tog, 2 dc) 6 times (30 sts).
Round 22: (3 dc, dc2tog) 6 times (24 sts).
Round 23: (Dc, dc2tog, dc) 6 times (18 sts).
Round 24: (Dc, dc2tog) 6 times (12 sts).
Round 25: (Dc, dc2tog) 4 times (8 sts).
Fasten off and weave the yarn under each of the FLO, pull tight and hide the end inside the head.

MAKING UP

BEAK

Pin the beak to the front of the face, centred between the safety eyes at round 12. There should be 1 stitch on each side of the beak before the safety eyes. When it looks even, attach it with whip stitches using the large embroidery needle and weave in the end.

HEAD AND BODY

Before attaching the head to the body, use pins to ensure the placement is correct. You want the centre of the base of the head to be slightly forward to add the look of a larger chin. Make sure the back of the head is centred with the tail. Attach the head and body by using the large embroidery needle and the long tail left over from the body to whip stitch the two together. Weave in the end when finished.

EYES

Outline the safety eyes inserted on round 13 of the head using the small embroidery needle and white and black crochet thread (see page 24).

WINGS

The wings will need to be pinned to get the right placement. They should be sewn 4 rounds down from the head between rounds 21 and 22 on the sides of the body, approximately 11 stitches apart. Slightly angle them down towards the tail before sewing. Attach with whip stitches using the large embroidery needle when they are even. Once sewn, add a few extra whip stitches to the bottom of the wings to ensure they stay secured and in that position. When complete, secure and weave in the end.

FEET

The feet should be pinned between rounds 6 and 9 of the front of the body, with 4 stitches between them and the htr stitches facing down. This position will angle the feet forward. Make sure the heels are touching the flat surface it is on so it will sit properly. If not, adjust the feet up or down a round to ensure a good sitting position. Then, using the large embroidery needle, attach the feet to the body with whip stitches. When complete, secure and weave in the end.

Hazel the Cow

Hazel can't wait to grow up and make milk for all the boys and girls who visit the farm, just like her mother and aunts do every day. One day, Farmer Ed will give her a beautiful bell to hang around her neck and she will be a full-grown dairy cow! Until then, she will just have to keep making faces at the piglets and playing peek-a-boo with the bunnies.

Skill level

Finished size

6in (15cm)

Supplies and materials

Lion Brand Mandala Ombré, 100% acrylic (344yd/315m per 150g)

1 ball in Zen

Size 10 crochet thread in black and white

2.75mm (US C/2) crochet hook

2 x ½in (12mm) safety eyes

Polyester fibre filling

Large and small embroidery needles

Scissors

Sewing pins

Stitch markers

With this pattern, there will be colour changes for the spots. Start by cutting out the chosen colour in the yarn cake for the cow's spots and set it aside. We will call this colour B. Crochet the muzzle and hooves using the next colour. Pull from the colour on the outside or the inside of the yarn cake at the centre pull. Then continue the rest of the body in the other continuous ombré colours from the beginning to the end of the pattern with alternating colour changes for the spots.

Starting with either the inside or the outside of the yarn cake, work all the stitches in a round unless otherwise instructed.

MUZZLE

Round 1: Make a MC with 6 dc (6 sts).
Round 2: (Dc2inc) 6 times (12 sts).
Round 3: (Dc, dc2inc) 6 times (18 sts).
Round 4: (Dc, dc2inc, dc) 6 times (24 sts).
Round 5: (3 dc, dc2inc) 6 times (30 sts).
Round 6: (2 dc, dc2inc, 2 dc) 6 times (36 sts).
Round 7: (5 dc, dc2inc) 6 times (42 sts).
Rounds 8–11: Dc in each st around.
Leaving the last stitch unfinished, cut the yarn and set it aside for a colour change later.
Cut a 12in (30cm) piece of yarn and set it aside to make the nostrils later.

HOOVES (MAKE 4)

Continuing the current cake yarn colour, work all the stitches in a round.
Round 1: Make a MC with 6 dc (6 sts).
Round 2: (Dc2inc) 6 times (12 sts).
Round 3: (Dc, dc2inc) 6 times (18 sts).
Round 4: (Dc, dc2inc, dc) 6 times (24 sts).
Round 5: BLO dc in each st around.
Leave the last stitch unworked for the colour change step.
This will be the end of this colour. Cut any yarn left on the cake that needs to be trimmed off and set it aside. You will continue the next part with the next colour.

BACK LEGS (MAKE 2)

Connect the next yarn colour to the last stitch of the hooves and continue crocheting, working all the stitches in a round. Stuff as you crochet up to round 15.
Rounds 6–10: Dc in each st around.
Round 11: 6 dc, (dc2tog) 6 times, 6 dc (18 sts).
Rounds 12–14: Dc in each st around.
Round 15: (2 dc, dc2tog, 2 dc) 3 times (15 sts).
Rounds 16–17: Dc in each st around.
Pinch the leg closed. If your seam is not centred with the decreases on the hooves, add or subtract 1–3 stitches.
Dc through both sides with 7 dc and close the opening (7 sts).
Fasten off and leave a long tail for attaching.

BODY

Continuing the current cake yarn colour, work all the stitches in a round. Stuff as you crochet.

Round 1: Make a MC with 6 dc (6 sts).

Round 2: (Dc2inc) 6 times (12 sts).

Round 3: (Dc, dc2inc) 6 times (18 sts).

Round 4: (Dc, dc2inc, dc) 6 times (24 sts).

Round 5: (3 dc, dc2inc) 6 times (30 sts).

Round 6: (2 dc, dc2inc, 2 dc) 6 times (36 sts).

Rounds 7–12: Dc in each st around.

Round 13: (2 dc, dc2tog, 2 dc) 6 times (30 sts).

Rounds 14–16: Dc in each st around.

Round 17: (3 dc, dc2tog) 6 times (24 sts).

Rounds 18–21: Dc in each st around.

Round 22: (Dc, dc2tog, dc) 6 times (18 sts).

Rounds 23–24: Dc in each st around.

Round 25: (Dc, dc2tog) 6 times (12 sts).

Fasten off and leave a long tail for attaching.

. . . .

HEAD

Connect the continuing yarn colour to the last stitch of the muzzle and continue crocheting, working all the stitches in a round from bottom to top.

Stuff as you crochet.

Beginning on round 12 through round 16, you will switch between the current yarn colour and the spot colour you cut at the start of the pattern.

Round 12: BLO 23 dc, 5 dc with colour B, 14 dc (42 sts).

Round 13: 15 dc, 1 ch, skip 1 dc, 6 dc, (4 dc, 1 ch, skip 1 dc, 2 dc) with colour B, 13 dc.

Note: the chain spaces in round 13 are where you place the safety eyes later.

Round 14: 22 dc, 7 dc with colour B, 13 dc.

Round 15: 23 dc, 5 dc with colour B, 14 dc.

Round 16: 24 dc, 4 dc with colour B, 14 dc.

Round 17: (5 dc, dc2tog) 6 times (36 sts).

Add the safety eyes in the chain spaces on round 13.

Rounds 18–19: Dc in each st around.

Round 20: (2 dc, dc2tog, 2 dc) 6 times (30 sts).

Round 21: Dc in each st around.

Round 22: (3 dc, dc2tog) 6 times (24 sts).

Round 23: (Dc, dc2tog, dc) 6 times (18 sts).

Round 24: (Dc, dc2tog) 6 times (12 sts).

Round 25: (Dc2tog, dc) 4 times (8 sts).

Fasten off and weave the yarn under each of the FLO, pull tight and hide the end inside the head.

. . . .

EYELIDS (MAKE 2)

Continuing the current cake yarn colour, work all the stitches in a row. When crocheting in a chain, after turning, dc in the 2nd chain from the hook. Make 2 (1 in the current head colour and 1 in the spot colour).

Row 1: Ch 7, turn (7 sts).

Row 2: Dc in each st across (6 sts).

Fasten off and leave a long tail for attaching.

EARS (MAKE 2)

Continuing the current cake yarn colour for first ear and the spot colour for the 2nd ear, work all the stitches in a round. Do not stuff.

Round 1: Make a MC with 4 dc (4 sts).

Round 2: (Dc, dc2inc) twice (6 sts).

Round 3: (Dc2inc) 6 times (12 sts).

Rounds 4–5: Dc in each st around.

Round 6: (Dc, dc2inc) 6 times (18 sts).

Rounds 7–8: Dc in each st around.

Round 9: (Dc, dc2inc, dc) 6 times (24 sts).

Round 10: (Dc, dc2tog, dc) 6 times (18 sts).

Rounds 11–13: Dc in each st around.

Pinch the ear closed, dc through both sides with 9 dc, and close the opening (9 sts).

Ear 1 (right): Using the current yarn colour, fold the bottom of the ear, facing you to the centre of the 9 dc seam, and dc across once more (6 sts).

Ear 2 (left): Using the spot colour, fold the bottom of the ear, away from you to the centre of the 9 dc seam, and dc across once more (6 sts).

Fasten off and leave a long tail for attaching.

FRONT LEGS (MAKE 2)

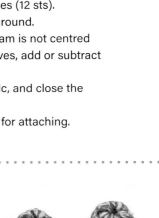

Connect the continuing yarn colour to the last stitch of the hooves and continue crocheting, working all the stitches in a round.

Stuff as you crochet up to round 18.

Rounds 6–10: Dc in each st around.

Round 11: 6 dc, (dc2tog) 6 times, 6 dc (18 sts).

Rounds 12–14: Dc in each st around.

Round 15: (2 dc, dc2tog, 2 dc) 3 times (15 sts).

Rounds 16–17: Dc in each st around.

Round 18: (3 dc, dc2tog) 3 times (12 sts).

Rounds 19–25: Dc in each st around.

Pinch the leg closed. If your seam is not centred with the decreases on the hooves, add or subtract 1–3 stitches.

Dc through both sides with 6 dc, and close the opening (6 sts).

Fasten off and leave a long tail for attaching.

HORNS (MAKE 2)

Continuing the current cake yarn colour, work all the stitches in a round.

Stuff as you crochet.

Round 1: Make a MC with 6 dc (6 sts).

Round 2: (Dc, dc2inc) 3 times (9 sts).

Rounds 3–4: Dc in each st around.

Fasten off and leave a long tail for attaching.

MAKING UP

EYES

Outline the safety eyes inserted on round 13 of the head using the small embroidery needle and white and black crochet thread (see page 24).

NOSTRILS

Before stitching, follow the next steps to place pins marking both nostrils and ensuring they are even with the safety eyes. Mark the nostrils 2 rounds down from the colour change between rounds 9 and 10, 3–4 stitches long and 3 stitches apart. Then, continuing the current cake yarn colour, make 2 horizontal whip stitches with the large embroidery needle where you marked the nostrils. Next, wrap the embroidery needle and yarn around the horizontal stitches until they are fully wrapped. When complete, secure and weave in the end.

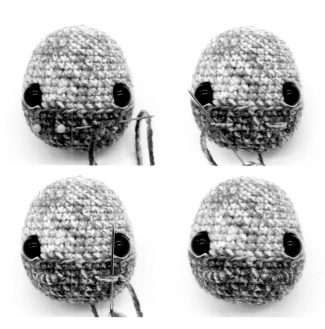

EYELIDS

Between rounds 15 and 16, use the large embroidery needle to whip stitch the inside corner of the eyelids with the wrong side facing up to the face. Attach the rest of the eyelid along the round for the length of 3 stitches. Continue down the outside of the safety eyes until the end of the detail on the safety eye between rounds 12 and 13. When finished, weave in the end.

EARS

Both ears should be placed on the side of the head 3 stitches away from the safety eyes, between rounds 19 and 20. The folds on each ear should be at the back of the head. Once the placement is correct, whip stitch them in place with the large embroidery needle. When finished, weave in the end.

HEAD AND BODY

Before attaching the head to the body, use pins to ensure the placement is correct. You want the head to be slightly forward to add the look of a larger chin. Once aligned, attach the head and body using the large embroidery needle and the long tail left over from the body to whip stitch the two together. When finished, weave in the end.

HORNS

Pin the horns directly on the head with 4–5 stitches between them and in front of the start of the ears. Once the placement is correct, attach the horns with whip stitches using the large embroidery needle. When complete, secure and weave in the end.

LEGS

Like all other parts, the legs need pins to get the correct placement before sewing. Each of the back legs should be sewn on the sides of the body, starting between rounds 5–6 and up to rounds 10–11. Make sure the cow can sit on its own before sewing. If not, adjust the legs up or down to achieve a perfect sitting position. Once even, whip stitch the legs to the body using the large embroidery needle. Then add a few extra whip stitches to the bottom of the legs to ensure they stay secured and in that position. Then, weave in the end.

The front legs should be pinned 2–3 rounds down from the head between rounds 23 and 24 and on the sides of the body. Leave at least 6–7 stitches between them on the back, and angle them slightly where the hooves touch the flat surface it is on. If the cow is sitting, start attaching the pieces with whip stitches using the large embroidery needle. If not, take this time to adjust the front legs up or down, to ensure a good sitting position. Add a few whip stitches to the lower and back portion of the front legs to secure the correct positioning, and weave in the end.

TAIL

Using 3 strands of the different colours of leftover scrap yarn about 6in (15cm) long, string the yarn through the lower back of the body between rounds 5 and 6. Gather all the yarn strands together and tie a knot with them up against the body.

Then group the 6 strands by 2s and make a braid that is approximately 2in (5cm) long. Add another knot at the end of the braid and trim any extra.

Aggie the Highland Bull

Aggie might just be the shaggiest little bull in the barnyard. Whenever anyone tells him they are too cold he just doesn't understand, thanks to his thick, bushy coat and the tuft of shaggy hair on top of his adorable little head. He likes to eat his grass and take naps underneath the large oak tree on the far edge of the pasture.

Skill Level

● ● ○

Finished size

6½in (16.5cm)

Supplies and materials

Lion Brand Mandala Ombré, 100% acrylic (344yd/315m per 150g)

1 ball in Cool

Size 10 crochet thread in black, white and gold

2.75mm (US C/2) crochet hook

2 x ½in (12mm) safety eyes

Polyester fibre filling

Large and small embroidery needles

Scissors

Sewing pins

Stitch markers

With this pattern, we start by crocheting the hooves, muzzle and horns from either the colour on the outside or the inside of the yarn cake at the centre pull. Then we continue the rest of the body in the other continuous ombré colours from the beginning to the end of the pattern.

Starting with either the inside or the outside of the yarn cake, work all the stitches in a round unless otherwise instructed.

Rounds 8-11: Dc in each st around.
Leaving the last stitch half worked and not finished off, cut the yarn and set it aside for a colour change later. Cut a 12in (30cm) piece of yarn and set it aside to make the nostrils later.

HOOVES (MAKE 4)

Round 1: Make a MC with 6 dc (6 sts).
Round 2: (Dc2inc) 6 times (12 sts).
Round 3: (Dc, dc2inc) 6 times (18 sts).
Round 4: (Dc, dc2inc, dc) 6 times (24 sts).
Round 5: BLO dc in each st around (24 sts).
Leaving the last stitch unfinished, cut the yarn and set it aside for a colour change later.

MUZZLE

Continuing the current cake yarn colour, work all the stitches in a round.
Round 1: Make a MC with 6 dc (6 sts).
Round 2: (Dc2inc) 6 times (12 sts).
Round 3: (Dc, dc2inc) 6 times (18 sts).
Round 4: (Dc, dc2inc, dc) 6 times (24 sts).
Round 5: (3 dc, dc2inc) 6 times (30 sts).
Round 6: (2 dc, dc2inc, 2 dc) 6 times (36 sts).
Round 7: (5 dc, dc2inc) 6 times (42 sts).

HORNS (MAKE 2)

Continuing the current cake yarn colour, work all the stitches in a round. Stuff as you crochet.
Round 1: Make a MC with 4 dc (4 sts).
Round 2: (Dc, dc2inc) twice (6 sts).
Round 3: Dc in each st around.
Round 4: (Dc, dc2inc, dc) twice (8 sts).
Rounds 5-6: Dc in each st around.
Round 7: 2 dc, (dc2inc, dc) twice, dc2tog (9 sts).
Round 8: 3 dc, dc2inc, dc, dc2inc, 3 dc (11 sts).
Round 9: 3 dc, dc2inc, dc, dc2inc, 3 dc, dc2tog (12 sts).
Round 10: Dc in each st around.
Round 11: 4 dc, dc2inc, 2 dc, dc2inc, 4 dc (14 sts).
Fasten off and leave a long tail for attaching.

BACK LEGS (MAKE 2)

Connect the current yarn colour to the last stitch of the hooves and continue crocheting, working all the stitches in a round.
Stuff as you crochet up to round 15.
Rounds 6-10: Dc in each st around (24 sts).
Round 11: 6 dc, (dc2tog) 6 times, 6 dc (18 sts).
Rounds 12-14: Dc in each st around.

Round 15: (2 dc, dc2tog, 2 dc) 3 times (15 sts).

Rounds 16-17: Dc in each st around.

Pinch the leg closed. If your seam is not centred with the decreases on the hooves, add or subtract 1–3 stitches. Dc through both sides with 7 dc and close the opening (7 sts).

Fasten off and leave a long tail for attaching.

FRONT LEGS
(MAKE 2)

Connect the continuing yarn colour to the last stitch of the hooves and continue crocheting, working all the stitches in a round. Stuff as you crochet up to round 18.

Rounds 6-10: Dc in each st around (24 sts).

Round 11: 6 dc, (dc2tog) 6 times, 6 dc (18 sts).

Rounds 12-14: Dc in each st around.

Round 15: (2 dc, dc2tog, 2 dc) 3 times (15 sts).

Rounds 16-17: Dc in each st around.

Round 18: (3 dc, dc2tog) 3 times (12 sts).

Rounds 19-25: Dc in each st around.

Pinch the leg closed. If your seam is not centred with the decreases on the hooves, add or subtract 1–3 stitches. Dc through both sides with 6 dc and close the opening (6 sts). Fasten off and leave a long tail for attaching.

BODY

Continuing the current cake yarn colour, work all the stitches in a round. Stuff as you crochet.

Round 1: Make a MC with 6 dc (6 sts).

Round 2: (Dc2inc) 6 times (12 sts).

Round 3: (Dc, dc2inc) 6 times (18 sts).

Round 4: (Dc, dc2inc, dc) 6 times (24 sts).

Round 5: (3 dc, dc2inc) 6 times (30 sts).

Round 6: (2 dc, dc2inc, 2 dc) 6 times (36 sts).

Rounds 7-12: Dc in each st around.

Round 13: (2 dc, dc2tog, 2 dc) 6 times (30 sts).

Rounds 14-16: Dc in each st around.

Round 17: (3 dc, dc2tog) 6 times (24 sts).

Rounds 18-20: Dc in each st around.

Round 21: (Dc, dc2tog, dc) 6 times (18 sts).

Rounds 22-24: Dc in each st around.

Round 25: (Dc, dc2tog) 6 times (12 sts).

Fasten off and leave a long tail for attaching.

HEAD

Connect the continuing yarn colour to the last stitch of the muzzle and continue crocheting, working all the stitches in a round from bottom to top.

Stuff as you crochet.

Round 12: Dc in BLO in each st around (42 sts).

Round 13: 15 dc, 1 ch, skip 1 dc, 10 dc, 1 ch, skip 1 dc, 15 dc (42 sts).

Note: the chain spaces in round 13 are where you place the safety eyes later.

Rounds 14–16: Dc in each st around.

Round 17: (5 dc, dc2tog) 6 times (36 sts).

Rounds 18–19: Dc in each st around.

Add the safety eyes in the chain spaces on round 13.

Round 20: (2 dc, dc2tog, 2 dc) 6 times (30 sts).

Round 21: Dc in each st around.

Round 22: (3 dc, dc2tog) 6 times (24 sts).

Round 23: (Dc, dc2tog, dc) 6 times (18 sts).

Round 24: (Dc, dc2tog) 6 times (12 sts).

Round 25: (Dc2tog, dc) 4 times (8 sts).

Fasten off and weave the yarn under each of the FLO, pull tight, and hide the end inside the head.

EARS (MAKE 2)

Continuing the current cake yarn colour, work all the stitches in a round. Do not stuff.

Round 1: Make a MC with 4 dc (4 sts).

Round 2: (Dc, dc2inc) twice (6 sts).

Round 3: (Dc2inc) 6 times (12 sts).

Rounds 4–5: Dc in each st around.

Round 6: (Dc, dc2inc) 6 times (18 sts).

Rounds 7–8: Dc in each st around.

Round 9: (Dc, dc2inc, dc) 6 times (24 sts).

Round 10: (Dc, dc2tog, dc) 6 times (18 sts).

Rounds 11–13: Dc in each st around.

Pinch the ear closed, dc through both sides with 9 dc, and close the opening (9 sts).

Ear 1: Fold the bottom of the ear facing you to the centre of the 9 dc seam and dc across once more (6 sts).

Ear 2: Fold the bottom of the ear away from you to the centre of the 9 dc seam and dc across once more (6 sts).

Fasten off and leave a long tail for attaching.

EYELIDS (MAKE 2)

Continuing the current cake yarn colour, work all the stitches in a row. When crocheting in a chain, after turning, dc in the 2nd chain from the hook.

Row 1: Ch 7, turn (7 sts).

Row 2: Dc in each st across (6 sts).

Fasten off and leave a long tail for attaching.

NOSE RING

Using the gold crochet thread, work all the stitches in a chain. When crocheting in a chain, after turning, dc in the 2nd chain from the hook.

Row 1: 12 dc, turn.

Row 2: 11 dc (11 sts).

Fasten off and leave a long tail for attaching.

MAKING UP

EYES

Outline the safety eyes inserted on round 13 of the head using the small embroidery needle and white and black crochet thread (see page 24).

EYELIDS

Between rounds 15 and 16, one round above the safety eyes and the wrong side facing up, use the large embroidery needle to whip stitch the inside corner of the eyelids to the face. Attach the rest of the eyelid in a curved shape reaching between rounds 16 and 17 above the safety eye and ending at the stitch next to the outside white eye detail on the safety eye. When finished, weave in the end.

NOSTRILS

Follow the next steps to place pins marking both nostrils and ensuring they are even with the safety eyes. Mark the nostrils 2 rounds down from the colour change between rounds 9 and 10, 3–4 stitches long and 3 stitches apart. Then, continuing the current cake yarn colour, make 2 horizontal whip stitches with the large embroidery needle where you marked the nostrils with the pins. Next, wrap the embroidery needle and yarn around the horizontal stitches until they are fully wrapped. When complete, secure and weave in the end.

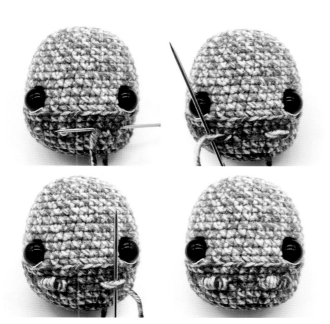

NOSE RING

Pin the nose ring under the centre of each nostril. Once the placement is right, whip stitch it in place using the small embroidery needle. When finished, weave in the end.

EARS

Both ears should be placed on the side of the head 2 stitches away from the eyelids starting at between rounds 20 and 21. With the folds facing forwards, angle each ear down towards the back and end at round 17 or 18. Make sure the fold in each ear is facing the front of the head. Once the placement is right, whip stitch it in place with the large embroidery needle. When finished, weave in the end.

HORNS

Pin the horns between the ears with 3 stitches between them. Make sure to have the horns pointing upwards and to the centre of the head. Then, with the large embroidery needle, attach the horns using whip stitches once the placement is correct. When complete, secure and weave in the end.

HAIR

The hair is attached by using the loop and hook method (see page 23). Start by cutting approximately 40 strands of the current cake yarn colour, 6in (15cm) long. Begin adding each strand of yarn starting at between rounds 23 and 24 of the front of the head. Continue adding hair between the ears and horns, stopping at the horns on the back of the head. Cut more strands if they are needed. Once all the hair is complete, trim the hair with scissors to 1½in (4cm) in length. The hair will fall in the middle of the safety eyes to create a tousled look.

HEAD AND BODY

Before attaching the head to the body, use pins to ensure the placement is correct. You want the head to be slightly forward to create the look of a larger chin. Once you are happy with the placement of the head, attach the head and body by using the large embroidery needle and the long tail left over from the body to whip stitch the two parts together. When finished, weave in the end.

LEGS

Like all other parts, the legs need pins to get the correct placement before sewing. Each of the back legs should be sewn on the sides of the body, starting between rounds 5–6 and up to rounds 11–12. Make sure the bull can sit on his own before sewing. If not, adjust the legs up or down to achieve a perfect sitting position. Once even, whip stitch the legs to the body using the large embroidery needle. Add a few extra whip stitches to the bottom of the legs to ensure they stay secured and in that position. Then, weave in the end.

The front legs should be pinned 2–3 rounds down from the head between rounds 23 and 24 and on the sides of the body. Leave at least 6–7 stitches between them on the back, and angle them slightly where the hooves touch the flat surface it is on. If he is sitting, whip stitch the front legs to the body using the large embroidery needle. If not, take this time to adjust the front legs up or down, to ensure a good sitting position. Add a few whip stitches to the lower and back portion of the front legs to secure the correct positioning, and weave in the end.

TAIL

Using 3 strands of the different colours of leftover scrap yarn about 6in (15cm) long, string the yarn through the lower back of the body between rounds 5 and 6 with the large embroidery needle. Gather all the yarn strands together and tie a knot with them up against the body. Then group the 6 strands by 2s and make a braid that is approximately 2in (5cm) long. Add another knot at the end of the braid and trim any extra.

Tillie the lamb

This is Tillie. She is very good at two things: eating all her dinner and escaping her pasture. To date, she has managed to get out five times and explore the farm. So far, her favourite place has been the pond, where she watched the frogs hop around the lilypads all afternoon.

Skill Level

● ● ●

Finished size

5in (12.5cm)

Supplies and materials

Lion Brand Mandala Ombré, 100% acrylic (344yd/315m per 150g)

1 ball in Felicity

Size 10 crochet thread in black, white and pink

2.75mm (US C/2) crochet hook

2 x ½in (12mm) safety eyes

Polyester fibre filling

Large and small embroidery needles

Sewing pins

Stitch marker

Scissors

The lamb is made by choosing the colours from the yarn cake's centre pull or the outside starting pull. The first colour will be for the head and hooves. Then end the colour by cutting the yarn and continuing the lamb with the next set of colours. Last, the ears will be made in a third colour.

Starting with either the inside or the outside of the cake, work all the stitches in a round unless otherwise instructed.

HEAD

Work all the stitches in a round from bottom to top. Stuff as you crochet.

Round 1: Make a MC with 6 dc (6 sts).
Round 2: (Dc2inc) 6 times (12 sts).
Round 3: (Dc, dc2inc) 6 times (18 sts).
Round 4: (Dc, dc2inc, dc) 6 times (24 sts).
Round 5: (3 dc, dc2inc) 6 times (30 sts).
Round 6: (2 dc, dc2inc, 2 dc) 6 times (36 sts).
Round 7: (5 dc, dc2inc) 6 times (42 sts).
Rounds 8–12: Dc in each st around.
Round 13: 15 dc, 1 ch, skip 1 dc, 10 dc, 1 ch, skip 1 dc, 15 dc (42 sts).
Note: the chain spaces in round 13 are where you place the safety eyes later.
Rounds 14–16: Dc in each st around.
Round 17: (5 dc, dc2tog) 6 times (36 sts).
Add the safety eyes in the chain spaces on round 13.
Round 18: Dc in each st around.
Round 19: (2 dc, dc2tog, 2 dc) 6 times (30 sts).
Round 20: (3 dc, dc2tog) 6 times (24 sts).
Round 21: (Dc, dc2tog, dc) 6 times (18 sts).
Round 22: (Dc, dc2tog) 6 times (12 sts).
Round 23: (Dc, dc2tog) 4 times (8 sts).
Fasten off and weave the yarn under each of the FLO, pull tight and hide the end inside the head.

HOOVES (MAKE 4)

Continuing the current cake yarn colour, work all the stitches in a round.
Round 1: Make a MC with 6 dc (6 sts).
Round 2: (Dc2inc) 6 times (12 sts).
Round 3: BLO dc in each st around.
Leaving the last stitch unfinished, cut the yarn and set it aside for a colour change later.
If the ending colour on the last hoof is still the starting colour, trim off the rest of that yarn colour and set it aside.
If the yarn colour changed on the last hoof, continue the next part with that colour.

LEGS (MAKE 2)

Connect the next yarn colour to the last stitch of the hooves and continue crocheting, working all the stitches in a round. Stuff as you crochet.
Rounds 4–7: Dc in each st around.
Fasten off and leave a long tail for attaching.

BODY

Continuing the current cake yarn colour, work all the stitches in a round. Stuff as you crochet.
Round 1: Make a MC with 6 dc (6 sts).
Round 2: (Dc2inc) 6 times (12 sts).
Round 3: (Dc, dc2inc) 6 times (18 sts).
Round 4: (Dc, dc2inc, dc) 6 times (24 sts).
Round 5: (3 dc, dc2inc) 6 times (30 sts).

Round 6: (2 dc, dc2inc, 2 dc) 6 times (36 sts).
Round 7: (5 dc, dc2inc) 6 times (42 sts).
Round 8: (3 dc, dc2inc, 3 dc) 6 times (48 sts).
Round 9: (3 dc, POP) 12 times.
Round 10: Dc in each st around.
Round 11: Dc, POP, (3 dc, POP) 11 times, 2 dc.
Round 12: Dc in each st around.
Round 13: (3 dc, POP) 12 times.
Round 14: Dc in each st around.
Round 15: Dc, POP, (3 dc, POP) 11 times, 2 dc.
Round 16: (3 dc, dc2tog, 3 dc) 6 times (42 sts).
Round 17: (POP, 2 dc, POP, 3 dc) 6 times.
Round 18: (5 dc, dc2tog) 6 times (36 sts).
Round 19: 11 dc, (POP, 2 dc) 3 times, POP, 15 dc.
Round 20: (2 dc, dc2tog, 2 dc) 6 times (30 sts).
Round 21: 10 dc, (POP, 2 dc) twice, POP, 13 dc.
Round 22: (3 dc, dc2tog) 6 times (24 sts).
Round 23: (Dc, dc2tog, dc) 6 times (18 sts).
Round 24: Dc in each st around.
Fasten off and leave a long tail for attaching.

ARMS (MAKE 2)

Connect the continuing yarn colour to the last stitch of the hooves and continue crocheting, working all the stitches in a round.
Stuff as you crochet up to round 10.
Rounds 4–14: Dc in each st around (12 sts).
Pinch the arm closed, dc through both sides with 6 dc, and close the opening (6 sts).
Fasten off and leave a long tail for attaching.

HAIR CAP

Continuing the current cake yarn colour, work all the stitches in a round.
Round 1: Make a MC with 6 dc (6 sts).
Round 2: (Dc2inc) 6 times (12 sts).
Round 3: (POP, dc2inc) 6 times (18 sts).
Round 4: (Dc, dc2inc, dc) 6 times (24 sts).
Round 5: (2 dc, POP, dc2inc) 6 times (30 sts).
Round 6: (2 dc, dc2inc, 2 dc) 6 times (36 sts).
Round 7: (POP, 4 dc, dc2inc) 6 times (42 sts).
Round 8: Dc in each st around.
Round 9: 2 dc, (POP, 2 dc, POP, 3 dc) 5 times, POP, 2 dc, POP, dc.
Round 10: Dc in each st around.
Fasten off and leave a long tail for attaching.

EARS
Inner ear (MAKE 2)

Continuing the current cake yarn colour, work all the stitches in a round.
Round 1: Make a MC with 6 dc (6 sts).
Round 2: (Dc2inc) 6 times (12 sts).
Round 3: (Dc, dc2inc) 6 times (18 sts).
Round 4: (Dc, dc2inc, dc) 6 times (24 sts).

Fasten off and hide the tails inside the inner ear.
Any continuing body colour yarn left on the cake needs to be trimmed off and set aside. You will continue the next part, with the next colour.

OUTSIDE EAR
(MAKE 2)
With the next cake yarn colour, work all the stitches in a round.

Round 1: Make a MC with 6 dc (6 sts).

Round 2: (Dc2inc) 6 times (12 sts).

Round 3: (Dc, dc2inc) 6 times (18 sts).

Round 4: (Dc, dc2inc, dc) 6 times (24 sts).

Rounds 5–6: Dc in each st around.

Place both the inside and outside parts of the ear together. Make sure both the wrong sides of each piece are facing each other.

Dc the next round through both pieces of the ear, making them into one complete ear.

Round 7: Dc in each st around.

Pinch the ear closed and dc across only the next 3 stitches, connecting both sides, closing the top of the ear and creating a small seam.

Fasten off and leave a long tail for attaching.

MAKING UP

EYES
Outline the safety eyes inserted on round 13 of the head using the small embroidery needle and white and black crochet thread (see page 24).

NOSE
Create an upside-down triangle nose using the small embroidery needle and the pink crochet thread. Apply 3 pins to outline the nose, beginning 1 round down from the safety eyes, 2 stitches wide, 1 round long, with 3 stitches between each safety eye and the pin. Pull your thread through the bottom of the head and out the top corner pin. Then, embroider a triangle from the top corner to the lower pin.

Continue moving your thread along the same round where the top corner pins are located and through the same bottom pin hole in a fan-like shape. Once finished, outline the top of the upside-down triangle with 3 whip stitches. Bring the needle back down through the head to where it entered. Tie the thread ends together and hide them within the head.

HAIR CAP
Pin the hair cap to the top of the head, 2 rounds above the safety eyes between rounds 16 and 17. Use enough pins to ensure the hair cap is centred and straight. Then, with the large embroidery needle, attach the cap to the head using mattress stitch. To make the first stitch, bring the needle under a stitch between rounds 16 and 17 of the head, up through the first stitch on the hair cap and down through the next hair cap stitch. Repeat these steps around the whole hair cap. Once the hair cap is completely secured around the head, weave in and hide the end.

EARS

Pin the ears to the edge of the hair cap approximately 4–5 stitches away from the safety eyes. The inside ears need to be facing the front of the head. Once the placement is correct, whip stitch them to the hair cap with the large embroidery needle. When finished, weave in the end.

HEAD AND BODY

Before attaching the head to the body, use pins to ensure the placement is correct. The head is centred, and the face is above the last round of popcorn stitches. It needs to be slightly forward to create the look of a larger chin. Once aligned, attach the head and body by using the large embroidery needle and the long tail left over from the body to whip stitch the two together. When finished, weave in the end.

LEGS AND ARMS

Pin the legs to the body starting at round 9. This is the first round of popcorn stitches at the lower front of the body. Fit each of them over the popcorn stitch straight down from the safety eyes, leaving 2 popcorn stitches between the legs. Whip stitch them in place with the large embroidery needle once the positioning is correct.

The arms should be pinned 1 round down from the head between rounds 23 and 24 and on the sides of the body above the popcorn sitches on round 17. Leave at least 1 stitch between them and the top round of popcorn stitches. Angle them slightly forward where the arms are almost parallel to the legs. If they are even, you can whip stitch the pieces to the body using the large embroidery needle. If not, adjust the arms up or down to ensure a good placement. When complete, secure and weave in the end.

Shawarma the Betta

Have you ever wondered what it's like to live underwater? Shawarma knows. Have you ever wondered what you look like from inside the aquarium? Shawarma knows! Have you ever wondered what it feels like to hide behind a big rock with your friends, come around the bubble treasure chest and then swim as fast as you can through the plants? Oh, Shawarma knows!

Skill Level

Finished size

6in (15cm)

Supplies and materials

Lion Brand Mandala Ombré, 100% acrylic (344yd/315m per 150g)

1 ball in Happy

Size 10 crochet thread in black and white

2.75mm (US C/2) crochet hook

2 x ½in (12mm) safety eyes

Polyester fibre filling

Large and small embroidery needles

Scissors

Sewing pins

Stitch markers

With this design, work the yarn cake from start to finish in a continuous motion. We will not be cutting the yarn and choosing colours.

Starting with either the inside or the outside of the cake, work all the stitches in a round unless otherwise instructed.

BODY

Work all the stitches in a round from nose to end.
Stuff as you crochet.

Round 1: Make a MC with 6 dc (6 sts).
Round 2: (Dc2inc) 6 times (12 sts).
Round 3: (Dc, dc2inc) 6 times (18 sts).
Round 4: Dc in each st around.
Round 5: (Dc, dc2inc, dc) 6 times (24 sts).
Round 6: Dc in each st around.
Round 7: (3 dc, dc2inc) 6 times (30 sts).
Round 8: Dc in each st around.
Round 9: (12 dc, dc2inc in the next 3 sts) twice (36 sts).
Round 10: Dc in each st around.
Round 11: Dc2inc, 7 dc, 1 ch, skip 1 dc, 4 dc, (dc2inc, dc) twice, dc2inc, 4 dc, 1 ch, skip 1 dc, 9 dc, (dc2inc, dc) twice (42 sts).
Note: the chain spaces in round 11 are where you place the safety eyes later.
Rounds 12–15: Dc in each st around.
Add the safety eyes in the chain spaces on round 11.
Note: to ensure the decreases starting in round 16 are centred on the top and bottom of the body, add or subtract a double crochet before the first set of decreases or after the last decreases only if needed.
Round 16: Dc2tog, 13 dc, (dc2tog, dc) twice, dc2tog, 13 dc, (dc2tog, dc) twice (36 sts).
Rounds 17–18: Dc in each st around.
Round 19: Dc2tog, 11 dc, (dc2tog, dc) twice, dc2tog, 11 dc, (dc2tog) twice (30 sts).
Rounds 20–21: Dc in each st around.
Round 22: Dc2tog, 9 dc, dc2tog in the next 3 sts, 9 dc, (dc2tog) twice (24 sts).
Round 23: Dc in each st around.

Round 24: Dc2tog, 6 dc, dc2tog in the next 3 sts, 6 dc, (dc2tog) twice (18 sts).
Rounds 25–27: Dc in each st around.
Round 28: Dc2tog, 3 dc, dc2tog in the next 4 sts, 3 dc, dc2tog (12 sts).
Round 29: Dc in each st around.
Pinch the body closed. If your seam is not centred with the safety eyes on the front of the face, add 1–2 stitches. Dc through both sides with 6 dc and close the opening (6 sts). Fasten off and weave the yarn end within the body.

TOP FIN

Work flat in rows.
Starting in row 2, after turning, work the next stitch down the chain and rows in the 3rd loop. The 3rd loop is the loop under the stitch. Using this technique brings the stitches to the outside of the fins on each side.
Note that the looser the tension, the easier it will be to grab the 3rd loop with your hook. Chains do not count as stitches.
Row 1: Ch 14, turn and work down the back of the ch. Starting in the next row until the last row, remember to

crochet in the 3rd loop under the stitch.

Row 2: Sl st in 2nd ch from hook, dc 12, ch turn (13 sts).

Row 3: Dc in the 3rd st from the hook, 7 dc, ch 3, turn (8 sts).

Row 4: Sl st in the 2nd st from the hook, dc in the next ch, 7 dc, ch, turn (9 sts).

Row 5: Dc in the 3rd st from the hook, 4 dc, ch 3, turn (5 sts).

Row 6: Sl st in the 2nd st from the hook, dc in the next ch, 4 dc, ch, turn (6 sts).

Row 7: Dc in the 3rd st from the hook, 2 dc, ch 3, turn (3 sts).

Row 8: Sl st in the 2nd st from the hook, dc in the next ch, 2 dc, ch (4 sts).

7 dc along the bottom edge to make a seam (7 sts).

Fasten off and leave a long yarn end for attaching.

BOTTOM FIN

Work flat in rows.

Starting in row 2, after each turn, work the next stitch down the chain and rows in the 3rd loop. The 3rd loop is the loop under the stitch. By using this technique, it brings the stitches to the outside of the fins on each side.

Note that the looser the tension, the easier it will be to grab the 3rd loop with your hook.

Chains do not count as stitches.

Row 1: Ch 18, turn and work down the back of the ch. Starting in the next row until the last row, remember to crochet in the 3rd loop under the stitch.

Row 2: Sl st in 2nd ch from hook, 16 dc, ch, turn (17 sts).

Row 3: Dc in the 3rd st from the hook, 11 dc, ch 3, turn (12 sts).

Row 4: Sl st in the 2nd st from the hook, dc in the next ch, 11 dc, ch, turn (13 sts).

Row 5: Dc in the 3rd st from the hook, 8 dc, ch 3, turn (9 sts).

Row 6: Sl st in the 2nd st from the hook, dc in the next ch, 8 dc, ch, turn (10 sts).

Row 7: Dc in the 3rd st from the hook, 5 dc, ch 3, turn (6 sts).

Row 8: Sl st in the 2nd st from the hook, dc in the next ch, 5 dc, ch, turn (7 sts).

Row 9: Dc in the 3rd st from the hook, 2 dc, ch 3, turn (3 sts).

Row 10: Sl st in the 2nd st from the hook, dc in the next ch, 2 dc, ch (4 sts).

10 dc along the bottom edge to make a seam (10 sts).

Fasten off and leave a long yarn end for attaching.

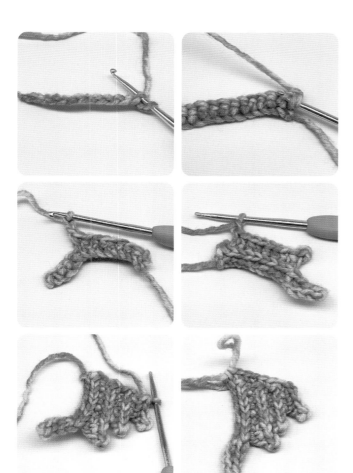

TAIL FIN

Work flat in rows.

Starting in row 4, after each turn, work the next stitches down the rows and chains in the 3rd loop. The 3rd loop is the loop under the stitch.

Note that the looser the tension, the easier it will be to grab the 3rd loop with your hook.

Chains do not count as stitches.

Row 1: Ch 18, turn and work down the back of the ch.

Row 2: Sl st in 2nd ch from hook, 15 dc, 3 dc in the last st (19 sts).

Continue working around the other side of the chain.

Row 3: 12 dc, ch 3, turn (12 sts).

Starting in the next row until the last row, remember to crochet in the 3rd loop under the stitch.

Row 4: Sl st in the 2nd st from the hook, dc in the next ch, 12 dc, 3 dc in the next st (17 sts).

Remember that the next row continues working around the other side, past the 3 dc in the last stitch.

Row 5: 11 dc, ch 3, turn (11 sts).

Row 6: Sl st in the 2nd st from the hook, dc in the next ch, 11 dc, 3 dc in the next st (16 sts).

Row 7: 10 dc, ch 3, turn (10 sts).

Row 8: Sl st in the 2nd st from the hook, dc in the next ch, 10 dc, 3 dc in the next st (15 sts).

Row 9: 9 dc, ch 3, turn (9 sts).

Row 10: Sl st in the 2nd st from the hook, dc in the next ch, 9 dc, 3 dc in the next st (14 sts).

Row 11: 8 dc, ch 3, turn (8 sts).

Row 12: Sl st in the 2nd st from the hook, dc in the next ch, 8 dc, 3 dc in the next st (13 sts).

Row 13: 7 dc, ch 3, turn (7 sts).

Row 14: Sl st in the 2nd st from the hook, dc in the next ch, 7 dc, 3 dc in the next st (12 sts).
Row 15: 6 dc, ch 3, turn (6 sts).
Row 16: Sl st in the 2nd st from the hook, dc in the next ch, 6 dc, 3 dc in the next st (11 sts).
Row 17: 4 dc, leaving the rest of the stitches unworked (4 sts). Fasten off and leave a long yarn end for attaching. Weave the beginning end into the bottom fin.

MAKING UP

EYES

Outline the safety eyes inserted on round 11 of the head using the small embroidery needle and white and black crochet thread (see page 24).

TOP FIN

On the top of the body, mark the top fin's location with pins starting between rounds 14 and 15 and ending at round 22. Make sure the fin is pinned with the first row at the top of the head and the last row near the back of the head. Centre the fin and align it with both of the safety eyes before sewing. Once the placement is right, whip stitch it on using the large embroidery needle.

BOTTOM FIN

Like the top fin, the bottom fin will need to be pinned to get the right placement before sewing. The bottom fin should be pinned starting between rounds 15 and 16 and ending at round 23. Make sure the fin is centred and aligned with both of the safety eyes before sewing. Once the placement is right, whip stitch on using the large embroidery needle.

TAIL FIN

The last row of the tail fin will be attached at the back of the body using the large embroidery needle. Angling the tail fin downwards, whip stitch the 6 stitches to attach the fin to the body giving the tail a fun flipping movement. Weave in any leftover ends within the tail and the body.

Daisy the Kitten

Daisy loves being a barn cat. There are mice to chase, dragonflies to swat at and Farmer Ed's wife, Nancy, leaves out dishes of cream for the kittens almost every day. Daisy's favourite thing is to sleep on the hay bales just inside the barn doors with the sun shining down on her and a soft breeze rustling her fur.

Skill Level

Finished size

5in (12.5cm)

Supplies and materials

Lion Brand Mandala Ombré, 100% acrylic (344yd/315m per 150g)

1 ball in Cool

Size 10 crochet thread in black, white and pink

2.75mm (US C/2) crochet hook

2 x ½in (12mm) safety eyes

Polyester fibre filling

Large and small embroidery needles

Scissors

Sewing pins

Stitch markers

The kitten is made by working most of the body in a continuous motion but then choosing an accent colour for one of the ears and the tail. By working the yarn this way, the last colour will stand out and give the kitten a fun colour scheme.

Starting with either the inside or the outside of the cake, work all the stitches in a round unless otherwise instructed.

HIND LEGS (MAKE 2)

Work all the stitches in a round.
Stuff as you crochet but do not overstuff the larger part.

Round 1: Make a MC with 6 dc (6 sts).
Round 2: (Dc2inc) 6 times (12 sts).
Round 3: (Dc, dc2inc) 6 times (18 sts).
Round 4: (Dc, dc2inc, dc) 6 times (24 sts).
Rounds 5-9: Dc in each st around.
Round 10: (Dc, dc2tog, dc) 6 times (18 sts).
Round 11: Dc in each st around.
Round 12: (Dc, dc2tog) 6 times (12 sts).
Round 13: Dc in each st around.
Round 14: 8 dc, 4 tr (12 sts).
Rounds 15-17: Dc in each st around.
Round 18: (Dc, dc2tog) 4 times (8 sts).
Fasten off and weave the yarn under each of the FLO, pull tight and leave a long tail for attaching.

FRONT LEGS (MAKE 2)

Continuing the current cake yarn colour, work all the stitches in a round. Stuff as you crochet.

Round 1: Make a MC with 6 dc (6 sts).
Round 2: (Dc2inc) 6 times (12 sts).
Rounds 3-10: Dc in each st around.
Pinch the leg closed, dc through both sides with 6 dc and close the opening (6 sts).
Fasten off and leave a long tail for attaching.

BODY

Continuing the current cake yarn colour, work all the stitches in a round. Stuff as you crochet.

Round 1: Make a MC with 6 dc (6 sts).
Round 2: (Dc2inc) 6 times (12 sts).
Round 3: (Dc, dc2inc) 6 times (18 sts).
Round 4: (Dc, dc2inc, dc) 6 times (24 sts).
Round 5: (3 dc, dc2inc) 6 times (30 sts).
Round 6: (2 dc, dc2inc, 2 dc) 6 times (36 sts).
Round 7: (5 dc, dc2inc) 6 times (42 sts).
Rounds 8-17: Dc in each st around.
Round 18: (5 dc, dc2tog) 6 times (36 sts).
Rounds 19-21: Dc in each st around.
Round 22: (2 dc, dc2tog, 2 dc) 6 times (30 sts).
Round 23: (3 dc, dc2tog) 6 times (24 sts).
Round 24: Dc in each st around.
Fasten off and leave a long tail for attaching.

HEAD

Continuing the current cake yarn colour, work all the stitches in a round from bottom to top.

Stuff as you crochet.

Round 1: Make a MC with 6 dc (6 sts).

Round 2: (Dc2inc) 6 times (12 sts).

Round 3: (Dc, dc2inc) 6 times (18 sts).

Round 4: (Dc, dc2inc, dc) 6 times (24 sts).

Round 5: (3 dc, dc2inc) 6 times (30 sts).

Round 6: (2 dc, dc2inc, 2 dc) 6 times (36 sts).

Round 7: (5 dc, dc2inc) 6 times (42 sts).

Rounds 8–10: Dc in each st around.

Round 11: 10 dc, (dc2inc) twice, 18 dc, (dc2inc) twice, 10 dc (46 sts).

Round 12: Dc in each st around.

Round 13: 10 dc, (dc2tog) twice, 3 dc, 1 ch, skip 1 dc, 10 dc, 1 ch, skip 1 dc, 3 dc, (dc2tog) twice, 10 dc (42 sts).

Note: the chain spaces in round 13 are where you place the safety eyes later.

Round 14: 10 dc, dc2tog, 18 dc, dc2tog, 10 dc (40 sts).

Rounds 15–16: Dc in each st around.

Add the safety eyes in the chain spaces on round 13.

Round 17: (4 dc, dc2tog, 4 dc) 4 times (36 sts).

Rounds 18–19: Dc in each st around.

Round 20: (2 dc, dc2tog, 2 dc) 6 times (30 sts).

Round 21: Dc in each st around.

Round 22: (3 dc, dc2tog) 6 times (24 sts).

Round 23: (Dc, dc2tog, dc) 6 times (18 sts).

Round 24: (Dc, dc2tog) 6 times (12 sts).

Round 25: (Dc, dc2tog) 4 times (8 sts).

Fasten off and weave the yarn under each of the FLO, pull tight and hide the end inside the head.

EARS (MAKE 2)

Continue the first ear in the current colour. Then cut any yarn left on the cake and set it aside. The second ear will be made in the next colour chosen as the accent colour. Work all the stitches in a round.

Do not stuff.

Round 1: Make a MC with 4 dc (4 sts).

Round 2: (Dc, dc2inc) twice (6 sts).

Round 3: (Dc2inc) 6 times (12 sts).

Rounds 4–6: Dc in each st around.

Pinch the ear closed, dc through both sides with 6 dc and close the opening (6 sts).

Fasten off and leave a long tail for attaching.

TAIL

Continuing the current cake yarn colour, work all the stitches in a round.

Stuff as you crochet.

Round 1: Make a MC with 5 dc (5 sts).

Round 2: (Dc2inc) 5 times (10 sts).

Rounds 3–34: Dc in each st around.

Pinch the leg closed, dc through both sides with 5 dc and close the opening (5 sts).

Fasten off and leave a long tail for attaching.

MAKING UP

EYES

Outline the safety eyes inserted on round 13 of the head using the small embroidery needle and white and black crochet thread (see page 24).

NOSE

Create an upside-down triangle nose using the small embroidery needle and the pink crochet thread. Apply pins to outline the nose beginning 1 round down from the safety eyes, 4 stitches wide, 2 rounds long, with 2–3 stitches between each safety eye and the pin. Pull your thread through the bottom of the head and out the top corner pin. Then embroider a triangle from the top corner to the lower pin. Continue moving your thread along the same round where the

top corner pins are located and through the same bottom pin hole in a fan-like shape. Once finished, outline the 2 bottom sides of the triangle and secure it at the bottom tip with a loop to complete the look. Bring the needle back down through the head to where it entered. Tie off and hide thread inside the head.

EARS

Ears are placed on the top of the back of the head starting between rounds 17 and 18 until round 22, 3 rounds away from the finished round. About 4 stitches will separate the ears before attaching. Once the placement is correct, and the ears are evenly placed, sew on using whip stitches and the large embroidery needle. When complete, weave in the end.

HEAD AND BODY

Since the kitten is lying down, pin the back of the head to the top of the body. Pin the body between rounds 7 and 13 of the back of the head. Make sure the head is centred. Once aligned, attach the head and body using the large embroidery needle and the long tail left over from the body to whip stitch the two parts together. When finished, weave in the end.

LEGS

Like all other parts, the legs need to be pinned to get the placement before sewing. The front legs should be 7 rounds down from the head between rounds 17 and 18, on the front of the body or the chest area and about 4 stitches apart. The legs will overlap the bottom of the head or at least touch it before sewing. Once even, whip stitch the front legs to the body using the large embroidery needle. When finished, weave in the end. Pin the larger portion of the hind legs to the sides of the body starting at round 7 and overlapping the front legs by 4 rounds. The trebles on the smaller portion of the legs need to be facing down with the leg parallel to the surface it is on. If the kitten is lying properly, you can start whip stitching around the back thigh part of the legs only using the large embroidery needle. If not, adjust the hind legs up or down to ensure a good position. When finished, weave in the end.

TAIL

The tail will be attached with whip stitches using the large embroidery needle to the bottom of the body to the right of the magic circle between rounds 2 and 3. Then, to keep it in place at the side of the body, add a few whip stitches to the tip of the tail and the front of one of the back legs. This ensures that the tail is permanently attached. Hide all the extra ends inside the body.

Jasper the Puppy

Jasper has grown up on the farm with his family and is learning to herd sheep like his dad and uncle. Right now though, the sheep don't listen to his little puppy barks and ignore him when he tries to run around and make them get into their pens at night. One day he will be a big dog, and those sheep will have no choice but to follow his instructions and move where he tells them to!

Skill Level

Finished size

6½in (16.5cm)

Supplies and materials

Lion Brand Mandala Ombré, 100% acrylic (344yd/315m per 150g)

1 ball in Harmony

Size 10 crochet thread in black and white

2.75mm (US C/2) crochet hook

2 x ½in (12mm) safety eyes

Polyester fibre filling

Large and small embroidery needles

Scissors

Sewing pins

Stitch markers

With this pattern, we start by choosing the colour of the nose and paws from either the colour on the outside or the inside of the yarn cake at the centre pull. Then we continue the rest of the body in the other continuous ombré colours from the beginning to the end of the pattern. We will not be cutting the yarn and choosing colours.

Starting with the inside of the cake, work all the stitches in a round.

MUZZLE

Round 1: Make a MC with 6 dc (6 sts).
Round 2: (Dc2inc) 6 times (12 sts).
Round 3: (Dc, dc2inc) 6 times (18 sts).
Round 4: (2 dc, dc2inc) twice, 6 dc, (dc2inc, 2 dc) twice (22 sts).
Round 5: (2 dc, dc2inc, dc2inc) twice, 5 dc, (dc2inc, dc2inc, 2 dc) twice, dc (30 sts).
Round 6: Dc in each st around.
Round 7: 14 dc, htr, (dtr, ch 2, sl st in the first ch, dtr) in the same st, htr, 13 dc (33 sts).
Fasten off, leaving a long tail for attaching.

PAWS (MAKE 4)

Continuing the current cake yarn colour, work all the stitches in a round.
Round 1: Make a MC with 6 dc (6 sts).
Round 2: (Dc2inc) 6 times (12 sts).
Round 3: Dc, dc2inc, (POP, dc2inc) 4 times, dc, dc2inc (18 sts).
Leaving the last stitch unfinished, cut the yarn and set it aside for a colour change later.

TAIL

Continuing the current cake yarn colour, work all the stitches in a round. Stuff as you crochet.
Round 1: Make a MC with 5 dc (5 sts).
Round 2: (Dc2inc) 5 times (10 sts).
Rounds 3–5: Dc in each st around.
Round 6: (2 dc, dc2inc, 2 dc) twice (12 sts).
Round 7: (3 dc, dc2inc) 3 times (15 sts).
Rounds 8–10: Dc in each st around.
Round 11: Dc, 7 htr, 7 dc.
Round 12: 8 dc, FLO 7 dc.
Round 13: Dc, 7 htr, 7 dc.
Rounds 14–24 even only: 8 dc, FLO 7 dc.
Rounds 15–25 odd only: Dc, 7 htr, 7 dc.
Round 26: 8 htr, 7 sl st.
Round 27: 8 htr, 1 sl st only (9 sts).
Fasten off, leaving a long tail for attaching.

BACK LEGS (MAKE 2)

Connect the continuing yarn colour to the last stitch of the paws and continue crocheting, working all the stitches in a round. Stuff as you crochet up to round 10.
Round 4: (Dc, dc2inc, dc) 6 times (24 sts).
Round 5: Dc in each st around.
Round 6: 6 dc, (dc2tog) 6 times, 6 dc (18 sts).
Rounds 7–9: Dc in each st around.
Round 10: (2 dc, dc2tog, 2 dc) 3 times (15 sts).
Rounds 11–13: Dc in each st around.
Pinch the leg closed. If your seam is not centred with the popcorn stitches on the paws, add or subtract 1–3 stitches. Dc through both sides with 7 dc, and close the opening (7 sts).
Fasten off, leaving a long tail for attaching.

FRONT LEGS
(MAKE 2)

Connect the continuing yarn colour to the last stitch of the paws and continue crocheting, working all the stitches in a round.
Stuff as you crochet up to round 18.

Round 4: (Dc, dc2inc, dc) 6 times (24 sts).
Round 5: Dc in each st around.
Round 6: 6 dc, (dc2tog) 6 times, 6 dc (18 sts).
Rounds 7–9: Dc in each st around.
Round 10: (2 dc, dc2tog, 2 dc) 3 times (15 sts).
Rounds 11–17: Dc in each st around.
Round 18: (3 dc, dc2tog) 3 times (12 sts).
Rounds 19–23: Dc in each st around.
Pinch the leg closed. If your seam is not centred with the popcorn stitches on the paws, add or subtract 1–3 stitches. Dc through both sides with 6 dc and close the opening (6 sts).
Fasten off, leaving a long tail for attaching.

BODY

Continuing the current cake yarn colour, work all the stitches in a round.
Stuff as you crochet.

Round 1: Make a MC with 6 dc (6 sts).
Round 2: (Dc2inc) 6 times (12 sts).
Round 3: (Dc, dc2inc) 6 times (18 sts).
Round 4: (Dc, dc2inc, dc) 6 times (24 sts).
Round 5: (3 dc, dc2inc) 6 times (30 sts).
Round 6: (2 dc, dc2inc, 2 dc) 6 times (36 sts).
Rounds 7–12: Dc in each st around.
Round 13: (2 dc, dc2tog, 2 dc) 6 times (30 sts).
Rounds 14–16: Dc in each st around.

Round 17: (3 dc, dc2tog) 6 times (24 sts).
Rounds 18–20: Dc in each st around.
Round 21: (Dc, dc2tog, dc) 6 times (18 sts).
Rounds 22–24: Dc in each st around.
Fasten off, leaving a long tail for attaching.

HEAD

Continuing the current cake yarn colour, work all the stitches in a round from bottom to top.
Stuff as you crochet.

Round 1: Make a MC with 6 dc (6 sts).
Round 2: (Dc2inc) 6 times (12 sts).
Round 3: (Dc, dc2inc) 6 times (18 sts).
Round 4: (Dc, dc2inc, dc) 6 times (24 sts).
Round 5: (3 dc, dc2inc) 6 times (30 sts).
Round 6: (2 dc, dc2inc, 2 dc) 6 times (36 sts).
Round 7: (5 dc, dc2inc) 6 times (42 sts).
Rounds 8–12: Dc in each st around.
Round 13: 15 dc, 1 ch, skip 1 dc, 10 dc, 1 ch, skip 1 dc, 15 dc.
Note: the chain spaces in round 13 are where you place the safety eyes later.
Rounds 14–16: Dc in each st around.
Round 17: (5 dc, dc2tog) 6 times (36 sts).
Rounds 18–19: Dc in each st around.
Add the safety eyes in the chain spaces on round 13.
Round 20: (2 dc, dc2tog, 2 dc) 6 times (30 sts).
Round 21: Dc in each st around.
Round 22: (3 dc, dc2tog) 6 times (24 sts).
Round 23: (Dc, dc2tog, dc) 6 times (18 sts).
Round 24: (Dc, dc2tog) 6 times (12 sts).
Round 25: (Dc, dc2tog) 4 times (8 sts).
Fasten off and weave the yarn under each of the FLO, pull tight and hide the end inside the head.

EARS (make 2)

Continuing the current cake yarn colour, work all the stitches in a round. Do not stuff.

Round 1: Make a MC with 5 dc (5 sts).
Round 2: (Dc2inc) 5 times (10 sts).
Round 3: Dc in each st around.
Round 4: (Dc, dc2inc) 5 times (15 sts).
Round 5: Dc in each st around.
Round 6: (Dc, dc2inc, dc) 5 times (20 sts).
Round 7: Dc in each st around.
Round 8: (3 dc, dc2inc) 5 times (25 sts).
Rounds 9–10: Dc in each st around.
Round 11: Tr, 11 dtr, tr, FLO 12 dc.
Round 12: Tr, 11 dtr, tr, 12 dc.
Rounds 13–14: Dc in each st around.
Round 15: (3 dc, dc2tog) 5 times (20 sts).
Round 16: Dc in each st around.
Round 17: (Dc, dc2tog, dc) 5 times (15 sts).
Pinch the ear closed. If the trebles and double trebles are not centred, add or subtract 1–2 stitches. Dc through both sides with 7 dc, and close the opening (7 sts).
Fasten off, leaving a long tail for attaching.

MAKING UP

EYES

Outline the safety eyes inserted on round 13 of the head using the small embroidery needle and white and black crochet thread (see page 24).

MUZZLE AND NOSE

Pin the muzzle between the eyes and centre on the face, with the pointed stitches positioned upwards. The point is equal to the top of the eyes between rounds 14 and 15 and the bottom of the muzzle is pinned at round 3 of the head. When your placement is correct, with the large embroidery needle, use whip stitches to attach and stuff the muzzle before closing the last stitches. Place pins to mark a triangle-shaped nose on the muzzle. The 2 top pins marked at round 4 are evenly spaced with 4 stitches between the bottom pin at the magic circle of the muzzle. Using the small embroidery needle and the black crochet thread, push your needle through the bottom of the muzzle. Taking it from the bottom point of the triangle, embroider a line to each of your pin markings. This will ensure the nose keeps its shape. Then, embroider the triangle nose in a fan-like shape working from one side to the other and along round 4. Once finished, outline the triangle to complete the look. Tie the thread ends together and hide them within the muzzle.

EARS

The ears are placed on the top of the head starting at round 20. The left ear is pinned 7 stitches from the left eye between rounds 17 and 18 and the right ear is pinned 6 stitches from the right eye between rounds 15 and 16. Make sure the ears are folded forward and then whip stitch them in place using the large embroidery needle. When finished, weave in the ends.

HEAD AND BODY

Pin the head on top of the body. The head needs to be slightly forward to create the look of a larger chin and tilted to the right with the magic circle parallel to the left side of the body. Once in a good position, attach the head and body by using the large embroidery needle and the long tail left over from the body to whip stitch the two parts together. When finished, weave in the end.

LEGS

Like all other parts, pin the legs to get the correct placement before sewing. The back legs should be between rounds 5 and 6 and 11 and 12, on the sides of the body and parallel to the ears. Make sure the puppy can sit on his own before attaching. If not, adjust the legs up or down for 1 or 2 rounds to get a perfect sitting position. Once even, whip stitch the legs to the body using the large embroidery needle. Add a few whip stitches along the bottom of the legs to ensure they are secured and don't move around. When complete, secure and weave in the end. Pin the front legs 1 round down from the head and on the sides of the body, leaving 7 stitches between them on the back of the top of the legs. Angle the front legs down to end just past the back legs. Make sure the paws touch the flat surface before sewing the pieces to the body. If not, adjust the front legs up or down a round to ensure a good sitting position. Whip stitch the front legs to the body using the large embroidery needle. Once sewn, add a few extra whip stitches to the back of the front legs to ensure they stay secured and in that position. When complete, secure and weave in the end.

TAIL

Attach the tail to the lower back between rounds 9 and 13 and centre between the back legs. Position the tail with the last round of half treble stitches to the left and the slip stitches to the right. This will curve the tail to the right of the body. Then, using the large embroidery needle, whip stitch it on once the placement is correct. When complete, secure and weave in the end.

Emilio the Axolotl

Unlike other creatures, Emilio never has to grow up. Luckily, as he lives in a permanently juvenile stage of growth, he can practise his skills at being the best little prankster the pond has ever seen!

Skill Level

Finished size

9in (22.5cm)

Supplies and materials

Lion Brand Mandala Ombré, 100% acrylic (344yd/315m per 150g)

1 ball in Pure

Size 10 crochet thread in black, white and pink

2.75mm (US C/2) crochet hook

2 x ½in (12mm) safety eyes

Polyester fibre filling

Large and small embroidery needles

Scissors

Sewing pins

Stitch markers

With this pattern, we start by choosing the colour of the gills from either the colour on the outside or the inside of the yarn cake at the centre pull. Then we end that colour by cutting the yarn and continuing the rest of the body in the other continuous ombré colours from the beginning to end of the pattern.

. . . .

RUFFLES

Starting with the darkest coloured yarn on the inside or outside of the cake, work all the stitches in a chain. These pieces will act like accent colours for the gills.

LARGE RUFFLE (MAKE 2)

Follow the steps below to make 3 sets of 3 points.
Ch 5, dc in the 3rd ch from the hook, (ch 4, dc in the 3rd ch from hook) twice, *ch 6, dc in the 3rd ch from hook, (ch 4, dc in the 3rd ch from hook) twice; rep from *, ch 2 (3 sets of 3 points).
Fasten off and leave a long tail for attaching.

SMALL RUFFLE
(MAKE 1)

Follow the steps below to make 5 points.
Ch 5, dc in the 3rd ch from the hook, (ch 4, dc in the 3rd ch from the hook) 4 times, ch 2 (5 points).
Fasten off and leave a long tail for attaching.
Any dark-coloured yarn left on the cake needs to be trimmed off and set aside. You will continue the next part with the next colour.

. . . .

BODY

With the next cake yarn colour, work all the stitches in a round from bottom to top.
Stuff as you crochet.
Round 1: Make a MC with 6 dc (6 sts).
Round 2: Dc in each st around.
Round 3: (Dc2inc) 6 times (12 sts).
Rounds 4-10: Dc in each st around.
Round 11: (5 dc, dc2inc) twice (14 sts).
Round 12: Dc in each st around.
Round 13: (3 dc, dc2inc, 3 dc) twice (16 sts).
Round 14: Dc in each st around.
Round 15: (7 dc, dc2inc) twice (18 sts).
Rounds 16-20: Dc in each st around.
Round 21: (Dc, dc2inc, dc) 6 times (24 sts).
Rounds 22-26: Dc in each st around.
Round 27: (3 dc, dc2inc) 6 times (30 sts).

Round 28: (2 dc, dc2inc, 2 dc) 6 times (36 sts).
Rounds 29–33: Dc in each st around.
Round 34: (2 dc, dc2tog, 2 dc) 6 times (30 sts).
Rounds 35–38: Dc in each st around.
Round 39: (3 dc, dc2tog) 6 times (24 sts).
Rounds 40–42: Dc in each st around.
Round 43: (Dc, dc2tog, dc) 6 times (18 sts).
Round 44: Dc in each st around.
Fasten off and leave a long tail for attaching.

BOTTOM LEGS (MAKE 2)

Continuing the current cake yarn colour,
work all the stitches in a round.
Lightly stuff as you crochet.
Round 1: Make a MC with 6 dc (6 sts).
Round 2: (Dc, dc2inc, dc) twice (8 sts).
Rounds 3–7: Dc in each st around.
Pinch the leg closed, dc through both sides
with 4 dc and close the opening (4 sts).
Fasten off and leave a long tail for attaching.

TOP LEGS (MAKE 2)

Continuing the current cake
yarn colour, work all the
stitches in a round.
Lightly stuff as you crochet.
Round 1: Make a MC
with 6 dc (6 sts).
Round 2: (Dc, dc2inc, dc)
twice (8 sts).
Rounds 3–9: Dc in each
st around.
Pinch the leg closed, dc through both sides with 4 dc
and close the opening (4 sts).
Fasten off and leave a long tail for attaching.

HEAD

Continuing the current cake yarn colour, work all the stitches in a round.

Stuff as you crochet.

Round 1: Make a MC with 6 dc (6 sts).

Round 2: (Dc2inc) 6 times (12 sts).

Round 3: (Dc, dc2inc) 6 times (18 sts).

Round 4: (Dc, dc2inc, dc) 6 times (24 sts).

Round 5: (3 dc, dc2inc) 6 times (30 sts).

Round 6: (2 dc, dc2inc, 2 dc) 6 times (36 sts).

Round 7: (5 dc, dc2inc) 6 times (42 sts).

Rounds 8–11: Dc in each st around.

Round 12: 15 dc, 1 ch, skip 1 dc, 10 dc, 1 ch, skip 1 dc, 15 dc (42 sts).

Note: the chain spaces in round 12 are where you place the safety eyes later.

Rounds 13–16: Dc in each st around.

Round 17: (5 dc, dc2tog) 6 times (36 sts).

Round 18: Dc in each st around.

Add the safety eyes in the chain spaces on round 12. Make sure the backs are fastened as far as they will push down on the stem of the safety eye. This will ensure that they will not move and will be tight enough for the details later.

Round 19: (2 dc, dc2tog, 2 dc) 6 times (30 sts).

Round 20: (3 dc, dc2tog) 6 times (24 sts).

Round 21: (Dc, dc2tog, dc) 6 times (18 sts).

Round 22: (Dc, dc2tog) 6 times (12 sts).

Round 23: (Dc, dc2tog) 4 times (8 sts).

Fasten off and weave the yarn under each of the FLO, pull tight and hide the end inside the head.

Trim off the rest of the current yarn colour and set it aside. You will continue the next part with the next colour.

GILLS (MAKE 6)

Starting with the new colour, work all the stitches in a round from top to bottom.
Do not stuff.

Round 1: Make a MC with 5 dc (5 sts).
Round 2: (Dc2inc) 5 times (10 sts).
Round 3: Dc in each st around.
Round 4: (Dc, dc2inc) 5 times (15 sts).
Gills 1-4: Fasten off and hide the end inside the gill.
Gills 5-6: For gills 5 and 6, DO NOT fasten off and instead continue to step 1.
Step 1: Pinch the opening of the gill closed and dc through both sides with 7 dc and close the opening (7 sts).
Step 2: With the last loop on the hook, insert your hook under 2 stitches of the 2nd gill and dc through both sides with 7 dc. This should have connected the 2 gills together.
Step 3: Repeat step 2 for the 3rd gill.
Fasten off and leave a long tail for attaching.

MAKING UP

EYES AND CHEEKS

Outline the safety eyes inserted on round 12 of the head using the small embroidery needle and white and black crochet thread (see page 24).

CHEEKS

Using the small embroidery needle and the pink crochet thread, push the needle through the bottom of the head. Then whip stitch a double line between rounds 10 and 11 below the safety eyes, starting near the end of the safety eye and 2 stitches wide. Once finished, bring the needle back down through the head to where it entered. Tie the thread ends together and hide them within the head.

GILLS

Pin ruffle 1 to the outside of the first set of gills. The pins should mark the ruffle's 2 ends, the 2nd point in each set of 3 at the top of each gill, and the 2 connecting spots. This will ensure your ruffle is sewn straight. After pinning, whip stitch ruffle 1 to the outside of each of the set of gills using the large embroidery needle. When finished, weave in the end. Then, pin the finished gills

to the sides of the top of the head starting between rounds 20 and 21 and leaving 3 rounds spaced on the top of the head between each of the first gills. Then pin the 2nd gill 6 stitches from the eyes. The 3rd gill needs to be parallel to the first gill on the top of the head and end at round 4 on the bottom of the head. When they look even, attach them with whip stitches using the large embroidery needle and weave in the end. Whip stitch ruffle 2 to the bottom of the body along the sides at rounds 1–7 using the large embroidery needle. There should be 6 stitches on the body between each end of the ruffle on the front and on the back of the body. Weave in the end when finished.

HEAD AND BODY

Before attaching the head to the body, use pins to ensure the placement is correct. You want the head centred on the body at round 3 with the gills parallel to ruffle 2. This will match up the last round of 18 stitches on the body and the 18 stitches on the head at round 3. Once you are happy with the placement, attach the head and body by using the large embroidery needle and the long tail left over from the body to whip stitch the two together. When finished, weave in the end.

The bottom legs should be pinned 9 rounds down from the head starting between rounds 36 and 37 and offset below the middle of the top legs. Angle them the same way the top legs are, toward the belly. Attach with whip stitches using the large embroidery needle when they are even. Add a few whip stitches along the back of the bottom legs to ensure they are secured and don't move around. When complete, secure and weave in the end.

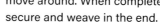

LEGS

Like all other parts, the top legs will need to be pinned to get the right placement before sewing. The top legs should be sewn 2–3 rounds down from the head on the sides of the body starting between rounds 42 and 43, just past the safety eyes. Leave at least 8–9 stitches between the tops of the legs on the front of the body. Slightly angle them down towards the belly. Attach with whip stitches using the large embroidery needle when they are even. Add a few whip stitches along the bottom of the top legs to ensure they are secured and don't move around. When complete, secure and weave in the end.

Jacques the Turtle

Meet Jacques! He's small in size but his dreams of exploring the whole ocean are HUGE! Ever since he crawled off the beach and into the ocean, he's wondered what else is out there. So far, he's seen a boat, three crabs, a plastic shark fin and a fish that puffed up into a ball when he swam close. He knows there is a whole ocean to explore and he can't wait to show it to you.

Skill Level

Finished size

5in (12.5cm)

Supplies and materials

Lion Brand Mandala Ombré, 100% acrylic (344yd/315m per 150g)

1 ball in Mantra

Size 10 crochet thread in black and white

2.75mm (US C/2) crochet hook

2 x ½in (12mm) safety eyes

Polyester fibre filling

Large and small embroidery needles

Scissors

Sewing pins

Stitch markers

With this pattern, we start by choosing the colour of the top shell from either the colour on the outside or the inside of the yarn cake at the centre pull. Then we end the colour by cutting the yarn and continuing the rest of the body in the other continuous ombré colours from the beginning to the end of the pattern.

Starting with the dark coloured yarn on the outside or inside of the cake, work all the stitches in a round. These pieces will act like accent colours for the top of the shell only.

. . . .

SHELL

Stuff as you crochet, but do not over-stuff.
This will help later for a flatter bottom shell.
Round 1: Make a MC with 6 dc (6 sts).
Round 2: (Dc2inc) 6 times (12 sts).
Round 3: (Dc, dc2inc) 6 times (18 sts).
Round 4: (Dc, dc2inc, dc) 6 times (24 sts).
Round 5: (3 dc, dc2inc) 6 times (30 sts).
Round 6: (2 dc, dc2inc, 2 dc) 6 times (36 sts).
Rounds 7–9: Dc in each st around.
Round 10: (5 dc, dc2inc) 6 times (42 sts).
Round 11: Dc in each st around.
Round 12: FLO htr in each st around.
Fasten off and hide the tail inside the shell.
Any dark-coloured accent yarn left on the cake needs to be trimmed off and set aside. You will continue the next part with the next colour.

Connect the next yarn colour to the BLO of round 11 and continue crocheting with this colour, working all the stitches in a round.
Round 13: BLO dc in each st around.
Round 14: Dc in each st around.

Round 15: (5 dc, dc2tog) 6 times (36 sts).
Round 16: (2 dc, dc2tog, 2 dc) 6 times (30 sts).
Round 17: (3 dc, dc2tog) 6 times (24 sts).
Round 18: (Dc, dc2tog, dc) 6 times (18 sts).
Round 19: (Dc, dc2tog) 6 times (12 sts).
Round 20: (Dc, dc2tog) 4 times (8 sts).
Fasten off and weave the yarn under each of the FLO, then pull tight. Bring the needle up through the top portion of the shell and out of the magic circle and pull. This will slightly flatten the bottom shell. Then bring the needle back through the shell and out near the colour change on the bottom shell. Leave a long tail for attaching.

HEAD

Continuing the current cake yarn colour, work all the stitches in a round from bottom to top. Stuff as you crochet.

Round 1: Make a MC with 6 dc (6 sts).

Round 2: (Dc2inc) 6 times (12 sts).

Round 3: (Dc, dc2inc) 6 times (18 sts).

Round 4: (Dc, dc2inc, dc) 6 times (24 sts).

Round 5: (3 dc, dc2inc) 6 times (30 sts).

Round 6: (2 dc, dc2inc, 2 dc) 6 times (36 sts).

Round 7: (5 dc, dc2inc) 6 times (42 sts).

Round 8: 10 dc, (dc2inc) twice, 18 dc, (dc2inc) twice, 10 dc (46 sts).

Round 9: 22 dc, (dc2inc) twice, 22 dc (48 sts).

Round 10: 10 dc, (dc2tog) twice, 20 dc, (dc2tog) twice, 10 dc (44 sts).

Round 11: 10 dc, dc2tog, 8 dc, (dc2tog) twice, 8 dc, dc2tog, 10 dc (40 sts).

Round 12: 14 dc, 1 ch, skip 1 dc, 10 dc, 1 ch, skip 1 dc, 14 dc.

Note: the chain spaces in round 12 are where you place the safety eyes later.

Round 13: 19 dc, dc2tog, 19 dc (39 sts).

Rounds 14–16: Dc in each st around.

Add the safety eyes in the chain spaces on round 12.

Round 17: (11 dc, dc2tog) 3 times (36 sts).

Round 18: Dc in each st around.

Round 19: (2 dc, dc2tog, 2 dc) 6 times (30 sts).

Round 20: Dc in each st around.

Round 21: (3 dc, dc2tog) 6 times (24 sts).

Round 22: (Dc, dc2tog, dc) 6 times (18 sts).

Round 23: (Dc, dc2tog) 6 times (12 sts).

Round 24: (Dc, dc2tog) 4 times (8 sts).

Fasten off and weave the yarn under each of the FLO, pull tight and hide the end inside the head.

FRONT FLIPPERS
(MAKE 2)

Continuing the current cake yarn colour, work all the stitches in a round. Do not stuff.

Round 1: Make a MC with 6 dc (6 sts).

Round 2: Dc in each st around.

Round 3: (Dc2inc) 6 times (12 sts).

Rounds 4–5: Dc in each st around.

Round 6: 4 dc, (dc2inc) twice, 6 dc (14 sts).

Round 7: Dc in each st around.

Round 8: 5 dc, (dc2inc) twice, 7 dc (16 sts).

Round 9: 14 dc, dc2tog (15 sts).

Round 10: 6 dc, (dc2inc) twice, 5 dc, dc2tog (16 sts).

Round 11: 7 dc, (dc2inc) twice, 5 dc, dc2tog (17 sts).

Round 12: 7 dc, 4 htr, 4 dc, dc2tog (16 sts).

Round 13: Dc2tog, 6 dc, dc2tog, 6 dc (14 sts).

Round 14: Dc in each st around.

Round 15: (Dc2tog) 7 times (7 sts).

Fasten off and weave the yarn under each of the FLO, pull tight and leave a long tail for attaching.

BACK FLIPPERS
(MAKE 2)

Continuing the current cake yarn colour, work all the stitches in a round. Do not stuff.

Round 1: Make a MC with 6 dc (6 sts).

Round 2: Dc in each st around.

Round 3: (Dc2inc) 6 times (12 sts).

Rounds 4-5: Dc in each st around.

Round 6: 4 dc, (dc2inc) twice, 6 dc (14 sts).

Round 7: Dc in each st around.

Round 8: 5 dc, (dc2inc) twice, 7 dc (16 sts).

Round 9: 5 dc, (dc2tog) twice, 7 dc (14 sts).

Round 10: 4 dc, (dc2tog) twice, 6 dc (12 sts).

Pinch the flipper closed, dc through both sides with 6 dc and close the opening (6 sts). Fasten off, leaving a long tail for attaching.

TAIL

Continuing the current cake yarn colour, work all the stitches in a round. Do not stuff.

Round 1: Make a MC with 6 dc (6 sts).

Round 2: (Dc, dc2inc) 3 times (9 sts).

Rounds 3-4: Dc in each st around.

Pinch the tail closed, dc through both sides with 4 dc and close the opening (4 sts). Fasten off, leaving a long tail for attaching.

MAKING UP

EYES AND NOSE DETAILS

Outline the safety eyes inserted on round 12 of the head using the small embroidery needle and white and black crochet thread (see page 24).

NOSE

Create a V-shape for the nose using the small embroidery needle and the black crochet thread. Use pins to mark the nose in the centre of the face beginning on the round below the safety eyes between rounds 10 and 11, 2 stitches wide, 1 round long, with 3–4 stitches between each safety eye and the pin. Enter your needle through the bottom of the head and out the top corner pin. Then, embroider the V from the top corner to the bottom pin, and to the other top corner pin. Once finished, bring the needle back down through the head to where it entered. Tie the thread ends together and hide them within its head.

HEAD AND BODY

Before attaching the head to the body, use pins to ensure the placement is correct. Place round 13 of the shell up against the back of the head at round 5. The bottom of the head and the bottom

of the shell need to be even. Once aligned, using the large embroidery needle, sew the head and body together with at least 5 whip stitches by using the long tail left over from the body. To secure the head so it isn't floppy, bring the needle up through the shell and out at round 8 above the rim, and stitch the shell to the back of the head between rounds 11 and 12 with a whip stitch. When finished, weave in the end.

BACK FLIPPERS

The back flippers should be pinned between rounds 13 and 14 of the shell, with 3 stitches away from the front flipper. Make sure you are attaching the flat edge of the flipper where you pinched and dc to close them with the curve facing forwards. Attach with whip stitches using the large embroidery needle when they are even. Once complete, secure and weave in the end.

FRONT FLIPPERS

Like all other parts, the flippers need to be pinned to get the right placement before sewing. With the large embroidery needle, use whip stitches to attach them below the colour change of the shell, between rounds 13 and 14, and with 1 stitch away from the head. Make sure you are attaching the small flat edge of the flipper to the body with the curve facing forwards. Once complete, secure and weave in the end.

TAIL

Pin the tail to the back of the lower shell centred between the front flippers between rounds 13 and 14. This should be the same rounds where the 4 flippers are attached. When it looks even, attach it with whip stitches and the large embroidery needle and weave in the end.

Mischa the Otter

Mischa is an otter pup who lives for fun winter adventures. After the first snowfall, she gathers up her best friends and they race to the top of the icy slope for a game of slip and slide. The fastest otter down the hill and into the crisp waters gets the biggest prize fish, but for Mischa, the prize is nothing compared to the thrill of the adventure!

Skill Level

Finished size

5in (12.5cm)

Supplies and materials

Lion Brand Mandala Ombré, 100% acrylic (344yd/315m per 150g)

1 ball in Felicity

Size 10 crochet thread in black and white

2.75mm (US C/2) crochet hook

2 x ½in (12mm) safety eyes

Polyester fibre filling

Large and small embroidery needles

Scissors

Sewing pins

Stitch marker

The otter is made by choosing the colours from the yarn cake's centre pull or the outside starting pull. The first colour will be for the tail and feet, creating an accent colour. Then we will end the colour by cutting the yarn and continuing the otter with the next set of colours. The rest of the otter will show the ombré colour changes from the bottom to the top of the make.

Starting with either the inside or the outside of the cake, work all the stitches in a round unless otherwise instructed.

. . . .

TAIL
Work all the stitches in a round. Stuff as you crochet.

Round 1: Make a MC with 5 dc (5 sts).

Round 2: (Dc2inc) 5 times (10 sts).

Rounds 3–10: Dc in each st around.

Round 11: (2 dc, dc2inc, 2 dc) twice (12 sts).

Rounds 12–14: Dc in each st around.

Round 15: (5 dc, dc2inc) twice (14 sts).

Rounds 16–17: Dc in each st around.

Round 18: (3 dc, dc2inc, 3 dc) twice (16 sts).

Rounds 19–20: Dc in each st around.
Pinch the tail closed, dc through both sides with 8 dc and close the opening (8 sts).
Fasten off and leave a long tail for attaching.

. . . .

FEET (MAKE 2)
Continuing the current cake yarn colour, work all the stitches in a round.
When crocheting in a chain, after turning, dc in the 2nd chain from the hook.

Row 1: Ch 9, turn.

Row 2: 7 dc, 3 dc in the end ch, in reverse side of ch work 6 dc, dc2inc, turn (18 sts).

Row 3: Dc in each st around, turn.

Row 4: 6 dc, (3 htr in the same st, sl st) twice, (3 htr in the same st), 6 dc, dc2inc (25 sts).
Fasten off and leave a long tail for attaching.

This will be the end of the first colour. Cut any yarn left on the cake that needs to be trimmed off and set it aside. You will continue the next part with the next colour.

. . . .

BODY
Continuing the current cake yarn colour, work all the stitches in a round. Stuff as you crochet.

Round 1: Make a MC with 6 dc (6 sts).

Round 2: (Dc2inc) 6 times (12 sts).

Round 3: (Dc, dc2inc) 6 times (18 sts).

Round 4: (Dc, dc2inc, dc) 6 times (24 sts).

Round 5: (3 dc, dc2inc) 6 times (30 sts).

Round 6: (2 dc, dc2inc, 2 dc) 6 times (36 sts).

Round 7: (5 dc, dc2inc) 6 times (42 sts).

Rounds 8–13: Dc in each st around.
Round 14: (5 dc, dc2tog) 6 times (36 sts).
Rounds 15–17: Dc in each st around.
Round 18: (2 dc, dc2tog, 2 dc) 6 times (30 sts).
Rounds 19–22: Dc in each st around.
Round 23: (3 dc, dc2tog) 6 times (24 sts).
Rounds 24–26: Dc in each st around.
Round 27: (Dc, dc2tog, dc) 6 times (18 sts).
Round 28: (Dc, dc2tog) 6 times (12 sts).
Fasten off and leave a long tail for attaching.

ARMS (MAKE 2)

Continuing the current cake yarn colour, work all the stitches in a round. Stuff as you crochet up to round 10.
Round 1: Make a MC with 5 dc (5 sts).
Round 2: (Dc2inc) 5 times (10 sts).
Round 3: Dc in each st around.
Round 4: 4 dc, BOB, 5 dc (10 sts).
Rounds 5–15: Dc in each st around.
Round 16: 2 dc, leaving the remaining stitches unworked (2 sts).
Pinch the arm closed, dc through both sides with 5 dc and close the opening (5 sts).
Fasten off and leave a long tail for attaching.

HEAD

Continuing the current cake yarn colour, work all the stitches in a round from bottom to top. Stuff as you crochet.
Round 1: Make a MC with 6 dc (6 sts).
Round 2: (Dc2inc) 6 times (12 sts).
Round 3: (Dc, dc2inc) 6 times (18 sts).

Round 4: (Dc, dc2inc, dc) 6 times (24 sts).
Round 5: (3 dc, dc2inc) 6 times (30 sts).
Round 6: (2 dc, dc2inc, 2 dc) 6 times (36 sts).
Round 7: (5 dc, dc2inc) 6 times (42 sts).
Rounds 8–11: Dc in each st around.

Round 12: (5 dc, dc2tog) 6 times (36 sts).
Round 13: 12 dc, 1 ch, skip 1 dc, 10 dc, 1 ch, skip 1 dc, 12 dc.
Note: the chain spaces in round 13 are where you place the safety eyes later.
Rounds 14–19: Dc in each st around.
Add the safety eyes in the chain spaces on round 13.
Round 20: (2 dc, dc2tog, 2 dc) 6 times (30 sts).
Round 21: Dc in each st around.
Round 22: (3 dc, dc2tog) 6 times (24 sts).
Round 23: (Dc, dc2tog, dc) 6 times (18 sts).
Round 24: (Dc, dc2tog) 6 times (12 sts).
Round 25: (Dc, dc2tog) 4 times (8 sts).
Fasten off and weave the yarn under each of the FLO, pull tight and hide the end inside the head.

EARS (MAKE 2)

Continuing the current cake yarn colour, work all the stitches in a round. Do not stuff.
Round 1: Make a MC with 6 dc (6 sts).
Round 2: (Dc2inc) 6 times (12 sts).
Round 3: Dc in each st around.
Round 4: (Dc, dc2inc) 6 times (18 sts).
Pinch the ear closed, dc through both sides with 9 dc and close the opening (9 sts).
Fasten off and leave a long tail for attaching.

MAKING UP

EYES

Outline the safety eyes inserted on round 13 of the head using the small embroidery needle and white and black crochet thread (see page 24).

NOSE AND WHISKERS

Create an upside-down triangle nose using the small embroidery needle and the black crochet thread. Use pins to outline the nose beginning 1 round down from the safety eyes, 8 stitches wide, 4 rounds long, with 2 stitches between each safety eye and the pin. Pull your thread through the bottom of the head and out the top corner pin. Then, embroider a triangle from the top corners to the lower pin.

Continue moving your thread along the same round where the top corner pins are located and through the same bottom pin hole in a fan-like shape. Once finished, outline the top of the upside-down triangle with 2–3 whip stitches. Bring the needle back down through the head to where it entered. Tie the thread ends together and hide them within the head.

EARS

Pin the ears to the side of the head between rounds 13 and 20. There should be at least 3–4 stitches between each safety eye and the tip of the ears. Position more toward the back of the head with 7 stitches between each ear on the back of the head. Once the placement is correct, use the large embroidery needle to whip stitch them to the head. Weave in the end when finished.

HEAD AND BODY

Before attaching the head to the body, use pins to ensure the placement is correct. Centre the head, matching up the last round of 12 stitches on the body and 12 stitches on the head at round 2. Attach the head and body using the large embroidery needle and the long tail left over from the body to whip stitch the two parts together. Weave in the end when finished.

ARMS

The arms need to be pinned to get the right placement before sewing. They should be sewn 1 round down from the head between rounds 27 and 28 on the sides of the body, with the bobble stitch positioned upwards. Slightly angle them down towards the feet before sewing. Once even, whip stitch the arms to the body using the large embroidery needle. Add a few extra whip stitches to the bottom of the back of the arms to ensure they stay secured and in that position. When complete, secure and weave in the end.

FEET

Pin the feet to the front of the body at rounds 5–15, with the heels touching. Have the toes angled outward, not straight up and down. Make sure the gap between the feet is lined up with the nose. With the large embroidery needle, whip stitch the feet to the body. When complete, secure and weave in the end.

TAIL

Attach the tail to the lower back between rounds 8 and 9 and centred between the arms. Position the tail upward, then whip stitch it on with the large embroidery needle once the placement is correct. When complete, secure and weave in the end.

Weatherly the Unicorn

Weatherly is a free-spirited unicorn who prances to her own rhythm. Her colourful coat and bold curls make her stand out among the others in the herd. Nevertheless, she is just as magical, if not more, with her confidence in knowing that not all unicorns are made the same.

Skill Level

Finished size

9in (22.5cm)

Supplies and materials

Lion Brand Mandala Ombré, 100% acrylic (344yd/315m per 150g)

1 ball in Happy

Size 10 crochet thread in black, white and gold

2.75mm (US C/2) crochet hook

2.00mm (US B/1) crochet hook

2 x ½in (12mm) safety eyes

Polyester fibre filling

Large and small embroidery needles

Scissors

Sewing pins

Stitch markers

The unicorn is made by choosing the colours for specific pieces of the design, using the first colour for the muzzle and the hooves, working the ombré for the body and finally using each colour left for the mane and tail.

Starting with either the inside or the outside of the yarn cake, work all the stitches in a round unless otherwise instructed.

MUZZLE

Round 1: Make a MC with 6 dc (6 sts).
Round 2: (Dc2inc) 6 times (12 sts).
Round 3: (Dc, dc2inc) 6 times (18 sts).
Round 4: (Dc, dc2inc, dc) 6 times (24 sts).
Round 5: (3 dc, dc2inc) 6 times (30 sts).
Round 6: (2 dc, dc2inc, 2 dc) 6 times (36 sts).
Round 7: (5 dc, dc2inc) 6 times (42 sts).
Rounds 8–11: Dc in each st around.
Leaving the last stitch half worked and not finished off, cut the yarn and set it aside for a colour change later.

FRONT HOOVES
(MAKE 2)

Continuing the current cake yarn colour, work all the stitches in a round.
Round 1: Make a MC with 6 dc (6 sts).
Round 2: (Dc2inc) 6 times (12 sts).
Round 3: (Dc, dc2inc) 6 times (18 sts).
Round 4: BLO dc in each st around.
Leaving the last stitch unfinished, cut the yarn and set it aside for a colour change later.

BACK HOOVES
(MAKE 2)

Continuing the current cake yarn colour, work all the stitches in a round.
Round 1: Make a MC with 6 dc (6 sts).
Round 2: (Dc2inc) 6 times (12 sts).
Round 3: (Dc, dc2inc) 6 times (18 sts).
Round 4: (Dc, dc2inc, dc) 6 times (24 sts).
Round 5: BLO dc in each st around.
Leaving the last stitch unfinished, cut the yarn and set it aside for a colour change later.
If the ending colour on the last hoof is still the starting colour, trim the rest of that yarn colour off and set it aside. If the yarn colour changed on the last hoof, continue the next part with that colour.

BODY

With the next cake yarn colour, work all the stitches in a round from bottom to top.
Make 2 legs then connect the legs at round 16 to continue the body.
Connect the next yarn colour to the last stitch of the back hooves and continue crocheting.
Stuff as you crochet.
Rounds 6–9: Dc in each st around.
Round 10: (Dc, dc2tog, dc) 6 times (18 sts).
Rounds 11–15: Dc in each st around.
Fasten off after round 15 for the first back hoof.
If on the 2nd back hoof, continue to round 16.
Round 16: Ch 3, join the first leg with a dc.
Continue around the first hoof with 18 dc. 3 dc along the 3 ch, then 18 dc around the 2nd hoof (42 sts).
Place a marker to remember that the starting point will be from the beginning of the connecting ch.
Continue on the front side of 3 ch.

Round 17: (3 dc, dc2inc, 3 dc) 6 times (48 sts).
Rounds 18–20: Dc in each st around.
Round 21: (3 dc, dc2tog, 3 dc) 6 times (42 sts).
Rounds 22–25: Dc in each st around.
Round 26: (5 dc, dc2tog) 6 times (36 sts).
Rounds 27–28: Dc in each st around.
Round 29: (2 dc, dc2tog, 2 dc) 6 times (30 sts).
Rounds 30–31: Dc in each st around.
Round 32: (3 dc, dc2tog) 6 times (24 sts).
Round 33: Dc in each st around.
Round 34: (Dc, dc2tog, dc) 6 times (18 sts).
Rounds 35–36: Dc in each st around.
Round 37: 5 dc only
Fasten off and leave a long tail for attaching.

HEAD

Connect the continuing
yarn colour to the last stitch
of the muzzle and continue
crocheting, working all the
stitches in a round from
bottom to top.
Stuff as you crochet.
Round 12: BLO dc in each
st around.
Round 13: 15 dc, 1 ch, skip 1 dc, 10 dc,
1 ch, skip 1 dc, 15 dc (42 sts).
Note: the chain spaces in round
13 are where you place the safety
eyes later.
Rounds 14–16: Dc in each
st around.
Round 17: (5 dc, dc2tog)
6 times (36 sts).
Add the safety eyes in
the chain spaces on
round 13.
Rounds 18–19: Dc in each
st around.
Round 20: (2 dc, dc2tog, 2 dc)
6 times (30 sts).
Round 21: Dc in each st around.
Round 22: (3 dc, dc2tog)
6 times (24 sts).
Round 23: (Dc,
dc2tog, dc) 6 times
(18 sts).
Round 24: (Dc,
dc2tog) 6 times
(12 sts).
Round 25: (Dc, dc2tog)
4 times (8 sts).
Fasten off and weave the yarn
under each of the FLO,
pull tight and hide the end
inside the head.

EARS (MAKE 2)

Continuing the current cake yarn colour, work all the stitches in a round. Do not stuff.

Round 1: Make a MC with 4 dc (4 sts).

Round 2: (Dc, dc2inc) twice (6 sts).

Round 3: (Dc2inc) 6 times (12 sts).

Rounds 4–5: Dc in each st around.

Pinch the ear closed, dc through both sides with 6 dc and close the opening (6 sts).

Fasten off and leave a long tail for attaching.

This will be the end of this colour. Cut any yarn left on the cake that needs to be trimmed and set aside. You will continue the next part with the next colour.

ARMS (MAKE 2)

Connect the next cake yarn colour to the last stitch of the front hooves and continue crocheting, working all the stitches in a round.

Stuff as you crochet up to round 15.

Rounds 5–9: Dc in each st around.

Round 10: (Dc, dc2tog) 6 times (12 sts).

Rounds 11–20: Dc in each st around.

Pinch the arm closed, dc through both sides with 6 dc and close the opening (6 sts).

Fasten off and leave a long tail for attaching.

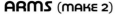

HORN

Use the 2.00mm crochet hook; the smaller hook creates a petite horn with fewer holes between the stitches.

With the gold-coloured crochet thread, work all the stitches in a round from bottom to top.

Stuff as you crochet.

Round 1: Make a MC with 12 dc (12 sts). Do not pull the string to the magic circle tight.

Rounds 2–3: Dc in each st around.

Round 4: (2 dc, dc2tog, 2 dc) twice (10 sts).

Rounds 5–6: Dc in each st around.

Round 7: (3 dc, dc2tog) twice (8 sts).

Rounds 8–9: Dc in each st around.

Round 10: (Dc, dc2tog, dc) twice (6 sts).

Rounds 11–12: Dc in each st around.

Round 13: (Dc, dc2tog) twice (4 sts).

Fasten off and weave the yarn under each of the FLO, pull tight and bring the thread down through the horn to use for sewing later.

HAIR

Starting the next cake yarn colour, work all the stitches in a row. After 2 rows, cut the yarn and switch to a new colour in the last stitch. When crocheting in a chain, after turning, dc in the 2nd chain from the hook.

Row 1: Ch 26, turn, dc in each st across (25 sts).

Rows 2–10: Ch 31, turn, dc in each st across (30 sts).

Rows 11–12: Ch 11, turn, dc in each st across (10 sts). Weave tails into each colour-matching row and twist the rows to create curls. Fold the hair in half at rows 5–6 to pair up the curls. Leave the last curls as singles, and do not pair them. Add a pin to hold them in place. Dc through both sides to create a top seam. Fasten off and leave a long tail for attaching.

TAIL

Choose 2 colours from the yarn cake to make the tail. When crocheting in a chain, after turning, dc in the 2nd chain from the hook.

Row 1: Ch 26, turn, dc in each st across (25 sts).

Rows 2–4: Ch 26, turn, dc in each st across.

Weave tails into each colour-matching row and twist the rows to create curls.

Fold the tail in half at rows 2–3 to pair up the curls. Add a pin to hold them in place.

Dc through both sides to create a top seam.

Fasten off and leave a long tail for attaching.

MAKING UP

EYES

Outline the safety eyes inserted on round 13 of the head using the small embroidery needle and white and black crochet thread (see page 24).

EARS

Pin both ears to the side of the head, between rounds 19 and 20, 2 stitches from the safety eyes. Once the placement is correct, whip stitch them in place using the large embroidery needle. When finished, weave in the end.

HORN

Attach the horn 5 rows above the safety eyes between rounds 19 and 21. Make sure to have the same number of stitches on the sides between the horn and the ears, ensuring your horn is centred and pointing upwards. With the small embroidery needle, use whip stitches to attach the horn. When complete, secure and weave in the end.

HAIR

Pin the hair directly behind the horn and down the back of the head to the muzzle. The hair should naturally fall to the left side of the head with the 2 shorter curls wrapped around the horn and in front of the ear. When centred, use the large embroidery needle to attach the hair with a mattress stitch and weave in the end.

HEAD AND BODY

Before attaching the head to the body, use pins to ensure the placement is correct. You want the head to be slightly forward to add the look of a larger chin. Attach the head and body by using the large embroidery needle and the long tail left over from the body to whip stitch the two together. When finished, weave in the end.

ARMS

The arms should be pinned 1–2 rounds down from the head between rounds 35 and 36 and on the sides of the body. Leave at least 5–6 stitches between them on the back, and angle them slightly towards the front of the body. Adjust the arms up or down to ensure an even placement and start to whip stitch the pieces to the body with the large embroidery needle. Add a few whip stitches to the back portion of the arms to secure the correct positioning, and weave in the end.

TAIL

Attach the tail at round 23 in the centre of the body. When centred, secure with a mattress stitch using the large embroidery needle and weave in the end.

Romeo the Donkey

Introducing Romeo the Donkey! He's a sweet boy who spends his days lounging in the fields, chasing butterflies and waiting for his Juliet to appear. Alas, so far, none have been taken with his messy hair and sleepy eyes. His best friend is Aggie the Highland Bull, and they like to play out by the large oak tree.

Skill level

Finished size

7in (17.5cm)

Supplies and materials

Lion Brand Mandala Ombré, 100% acrylic (344yd/315m per 150g)

1 ball in Chi

Size 10 crochet thread in black and white

2.75mm (US C/2) crochet hook

2 x ½in (12mm) safety eyes

Polyester fibre filling

Large and small embroidery needles

Scissors

Sewing pins

Stitch markers

With this pattern, start by choosing the colour of the muzzle and the hooves. The starting point can be from either the colour on the outside or the inside of the yarn cake at the centre pull. Then continue the rest of the body in the other continuous ombré colours from the beginning to the end of the pattern.

Starting with either the inside or the outside of the cake, work all the stitches in a round unless otherwise instructed.

MUZZLE

Round 1: Make a MC with 6 dc (6 sts).
Round 2: (Dc2inc) 6 times (12 sts).
Round 3: (Dc, dc2inc) 6 times (18 sts).
Round 4: (Dc, dc2inc, dc) 6 times (24 sts).
Round 5: (3 dc, dc2inc) 6 times (30 sts).
Round 6: (2 dc, dc2inc, 2 dc) 6 times (36 sts).
Round 7: (5 dc, dc2inc) 6 times (42 sts).
Rounds 8–11: Dc in each st around.
Leaving the last stitch half worked and not finished off, cut the yarn and set it aside for a colour change later. Cut a 12in (30cm) piece of yarn and set it aside to make the nostrils later.

HOOVES (MAKE 4)

Continuing the current cake yarn colour, work all the stitches in a round.
Round 1: Make a MC with 6 dc (6 sts).
Round 2: (Dc2inc) 6 times (12 sts).
Round 3: (Dc, dc2inc)

6 times (18 sts).
Round 4: (Dc, dc2inc, dc) 6 times (24 sts).
Round 5: BLO dc in each st around.
Rounds 6–9: Dc in each st around.
Leaving the last stitch unfinished, cut the yarn and set it aside for a colour change later.
If the ending colour on the last hoof is still the starting colour, trim off the rest of that yarn colour and set it aside. If the yarn colour changed on the last hoof, continue the next part with that colour.

BACK LEGS (MAKE 2)

Connect the next yarn colour to the last stitch of the hooves and continue crocheting, working all the stitches in a round. Stuff as you crochet up to round 10.
Round 10: Dc in each st around.
Round 11: 6 dc, (dc2tog) 6 times, 6 dc (18 sts).
Rounds 12–14: Dc in each st around.
Round 15: (2 dc, dc2tog, 2 dc) 3 times (15 sts).
Rounds 16–17: Dc in each st around.
Pinch the leg closed. If your seam is not centred with the decreases on the hooves, add or subtract 1–3 stitches.
Dc through both sides with 7 dc and close the opening (7 sts). Fasten off and leave a long tail for attaching.

FRONT LEGS
(MAKE 2)

Connect the continuing yarn colour to the last stitch of the hooves and continue crocheting, working all the stitches in a round.
Stuff as you crochet up to round 18.
Round 10: Dc in each st around.
Round 11: 6 dc, (dc2tog) 6 times, 6 dc (18 sts).

Rounds 12–14: Dc in each st around.

Round 15: (2 dc, dc2tog, 2 dc) 3 times (15 sts).

Rounds 16–17: Dc in each st around.

Round 18: (3 dc, dc2tog) 3 times (12 sts).

Rounds 19–25: Dc in each st around.

Pinch the leg closed. If your seam is not centred with the decreases on the hooves, add or subtract 1–3 stitches. Dc through both sides with 6 dc and close the opening (6 sts).

Fasten off and leave a long tail for attaching.

BODY

Continuing the current cake yarn colour, work all the stitches in a round. Stuff as you crochet.

Round 1: Make a MC with 6 dc (6 sts).

Round 2: (Dc2inc) 6 times (12 sts).

Round 3: (Dc, dc2inc) 6 times (18 sts).

Round 4: (Dc, dc2inc, dc) 6 times (24 sts).

Round 5: (3 dc, dc2inc) 6 times (30 sts).

Round 6: (2 dc, dc2inc, 2 dc) 6 times (36 sts).

Rounds 7–12: Dc in each st around.

Round 13: (2 dc, dc2tog, 2 dc) 6 times (30 sts).

Rounds 14–16: Dc in each st around.

Round 17: (3 dc, dc2tog) 6 times (24 sts).

Rounds 18–20: Dc in each st around.

Round 21: (Dc, dc2tog, dc) 6 times (18 sts).

Rounds 22–24: Dc in each st around.

Round 25: (Dc, dc2tog) 6 times (12 sts).

Fasten off and leave a long tail for attaching.

HEAD

Connect the continuing yarn colour to the last stitch of the muzzle and continue crocheting, working all the stitches in a round from bottom to top.

Stuff as you crochet.

Round 12: BLO dc in each st around.

Round 13: 15 dc, 1 ch, skip 1 dc, 10 dc, 1 ch, skip 1 dc, 15 dc (42 sts).

Note: the chain spaces in round 13 are where you place the safety eyes later.

Rounds 14–16: Dc in each st around.

Round 17: (5 dc, dc2tog) 6 times (36 sts).

Add the safety eyes in the chain spaces on round 13.

Rounds 18–19: Dc in each st around.

Round 20: (2 dc, dc2tog, 2 dc) 6 times (30 sts).

Round 21: Dc in each st around.

Round 22: (3 dc, dc2tog) 6 times (24 sts).

Round 23: (Dc, dc2tog, dc) 6 times (18 sts).

Round 24: (Dc, dc2tog) 6 times (12 sts).

Round 25: (Dc, dc2tog) 4 times (8 sts).

Fasten off and weave the yarn under each of the FLO, pull tight, and hide the end inside the head.

EARS (MAKE 2)

Continuing the current cake yarn colour, work all the stitches in a round. Do not stuff.

Round 1: Make a MC with 6 dc (6 sts).

Round 2: Dc in each st around.

Round 3: (Dc2inc) 6 times (12 sts).

Round 4: Dc in each st around.

Round 5: (Dc, dc2inc) 6 times (18 sts).

Rounds 6–7: Dc in each st around.

Round 8: (Dc, dc2inc, dc) 6 times (24 sts).

Rounds 9–10: Dc in each st around.

Round 11: (3 dc, dc2inc) 6 times (30 sts).

Rounds 12–15: Dc in each st around.

Round 16: (3 dc, dc2tog) 6 times (24 sts).

Round 17: Dc in each st around.

Round 18: (Dc, dc2tog, dc) 6 times (18 sts).

Rounds 19–20: Dc in each st around.

Pinch the ear closed, dc through both sides with 9 dc and close the opening (9 sts).

Fold the bottom of the ear in half and dc across once more (4 sts).

Fasten off and leave a long tail for attaching.

MAKING UP

EYES

Outline the safety eyes inserted on round 13 of the head using the small embroidery needle and white and black crochet thread (see page 24).

NOSTRILS

With pins, mark the nostrils 2 rounds down from the colour change between rounds 9 and 10, 3–4 stitches long and 3 stitches apart. Then, using the trimmed starting colour from the hooves and the large embroidery needle, make 2 horizontal whip stitches where you marked the nostrils with the pins. Once that step is complete, wrap the embroidery needle and yarn around the horizontal stitches until they are fully wrapped. When finished, secure and weave in the end.

EARS

Pin the ears to the side of the head between rounds 18 and 19. They will be slightly towards the back of the head, 4 rounds above the eyes and 6 stitches between them at the back of the head. Both ears should be facing outwards. When they look even, attach them using whip stitches and the large embroidery needle. Once sewn, add a few extra whip stitches to the back of the ears to ensure they stay secured and in that position, and weave in the end.

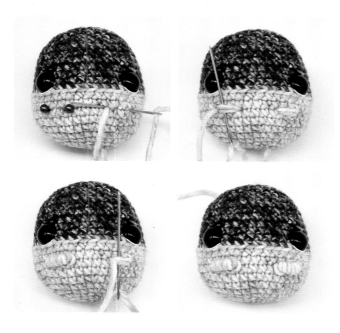

HAIR

The hair is attached by using the loop and hook method (see page 23). To start, cut approximately 50 strands of the current cake yarn colour, 6in (15cm) long. Begin adding each strand of yarn in short rows of 6 stitches starting at round 23 of the front of the head. Continue up between the ears and down the back of the head. Stop adding hair when the colour changes on the back of the muzzle. Cut more strands if they are needed. Once all the hair is complete, trim the hair with scissors to 1½in (4cm) long. The hair will fall in the middle of the safety eyes with a tousled look.

HEAD AND BODY

Before attaching the head to the body, use pins to ensure the placement is correct. You want the head to be slightly forward to create the look of a larger chin. Once you are happy with the placement of the head, attach the head and body by using the large embroidery needle and the long tail left over from the body to whip stitch the two parts together. Weave in the end when finished.

LEGS

The legs need pins to achieve the correct placement before sewing. Each of the back legs should be sewn on the sides of the body, starting between rounds 5 and 6 and up to rounds 10–11. Make sure the donkey can sit on his own before attaching. If not, adjust the legs up or down to get a perfect sitting position. Once even, whip stitch the legs to the body using the large embroidery needle. Add a few extra whip stitches to the bottom of the legs to ensure they stay secured and in that position. Then, weave in the end.

The front legs should be pinned 2–3 rounds down from the head between rounds 23 and 24 and on the sides of the body. Leave at least 6–7 stitches between them on the back, and angle them slightly where the hooves touch the flat surface the donkey is on. If he is sitting, whip stitch the front legs to the body using the large embroidery needle. If not, adjust the front legs up or down to ensure a good sitting position. Add a few whip stitches to the lower and back portion of the front legs to secure the correct positioning, and weave in the end.

TAIL

Using 3 strands of the different colours of leftover scrap yarn about 6in (15cm) long, string the yarn through the lower back of the body at rounds 5–6 with the large embroidery needle. Gather all the yarn strands together and tie a knot with them up against the body. Then group the 6 strands by 2s and make a braid approximately 2in (5cm) long. Add another knot at the end of the braid and trim any extra.

Neville the Alpaca

Neville can't wait for the summer! It's his favourite time of year, when all the alpacas get sheared for their wool. He gets hand-fed his favourite foods from over the fence – carrots and celery – and then he can roll in the grass and finally scratch his back!

Skill Level

Finished size

7in (17.5cm)

Supplies and materials

Lion Brand Mandala Ombré, 100% acrylic (344yd/315m per 150g)

1 ball in Zen

Size 10 crochet thread in black and white

2.75mm (US C/2) crochet hook

2 x ½in (12mm) safety eyes

Polyester fibre filling

Large and small embroidery needles

Scissors

Sewing pins

Stitch markers

With this pattern, we start by choosing the colour of the muzzle and hooves first from either the colour on the outside or the inside of the yarn cake at the centre pull. Then we continue the rest of the body in the other continuous ombré colours from the beginning to the end of the pattern.

Starting with either the inside or the outside of the cake, work all the stitches in a round unless otherwise instructed.

MUZZLE

Round 1: Make a MC with 6 dc (6 sts).
Round 2: (Dc2inc) 6 times (12 sts).
Round 3: Dc in each st around.
Round 4: (3 dc, 3 dc in the next st, dc, 3 dc in the next st) twice (20 sts).
Rounds 5-6: Dc in each st around.
Fasten off and leave a long tail for attaching.

HOOVES (MAKE 4)

Continuing the current cake yarn colour, work all the stitches in a round.
Round 1: Make a MC with 6 dc (6 sts).
Round 2: (Dc2inc) 6 times (12 sts).
Round 3: (Dc, dc2inc) 6 times (18 sts).
Round 4: BLO 7 dc, POP, 2 dc, POP, 7 dc (18 sts).
Leaving the last stitch unfinished, cut the yarn and set it aside for a colour change later.

BACK LEGS (MAKE 2)

Connect the next yarn colour to the last stitch of the hooves and continue crocheting, working all the stitches in a round.
Stuff as you crochet up to round 13.
Round 5: (Dc, dc2inc, dc) 6 times (24 sts).
Rounds 6-12: Dc in each st around.
Round 13: 8 dc, (dc2tog) 6 times, 4 dc (18 sts).
Rounds 14-17: Dc in each st around.
Pinch the leg closed. If your seam is not centred with the popcorn stitches on the hooves, add or subtract 1-3 stitches. Dc through both sides with 9 dc and close the opening (9 sts). Fasten off and leave a long tail for attaching.

FRONT LEGS (MAKE 2)

Connect the continuing yarn colour to the last stitch of the hooves and continue crocheting, working all the stitches in a round.
Stuff as you crochet up to round 18.
Round 5: (Dc, dc2inc, dc) 6 times (24 sts).
Rounds 6-16: Dc in each st around.
Round 17: (Dc, dc2tog, dc) 6 times (18 sts).
Round 18: (2 dc, dc2tog, 2 dc) 3 times (15 sts).
Rounds 19-21: Dc in each st around.
Round 22: (3 dc, dc2tog) 3 times (12 sts).
Rounds 23-25: Dc in each st around.
Pinch the leg closed. If your seam is not centred with the popcorn stitches on the hooves, add or subtract 1-3 stitches. Dc through both sides with 6 dc, and close the opening (6 sts). Fasten off and leave a long tail for attaching.

BODY

Continuing the current cake yarn colour, work all the stitches in a round. Stuff as you crochet.

Round 1: Make a MC with 6 dc (6 sts).

Round 2: (Dc2inc) 6 times (12 sts).

Round 3: (Dc, dc2inc) 6 times (18 sts).

Round 4: (Dc, dc2inc, dc) 6 times (24 sts).

Round 5: (3 dc, dc2inc) 6 times (30 sts).

Round 6: (2 dc, dc2inc, 2 dc) 6 times (36 sts).

Round 7: (5 dc, dc2inc) 6 times (42 sts).

Rounds 8-13: Dc in each st around.

Round 14: (5 dc, dc2tog) 6 times (36 sts).

Rounds 15-17: Dc in each st around.

Round 18: (2 dc, dc2tog, 2 dc) 6 times (30 sts).

Rounds 19-21: Dc in each st around.

Round 22: (3 dc, dc2tog) 6 times (24 sts).

Rounds 23-25: Dc in each st around.

Round 26: (Dc, dc2tog, dc) 6 times (18 sts).

Rounds 27-32: Dc in each st around.

Fasten off and leave a long tail for attaching.

HEAD

Continuing the current cake yarn colour, work all the stitches in a round.
Stuff as you crochet.

Round 1: Make a MC with 6 dc (6 sts).

Round 2: (Dc2inc) 6 times (12 sts).

Round 3: (Dc, dc2inc) 6 times (18 sts).

Round 4: (Dc, dc2inc, dc) 6 times (24 sts).

Round 5: (3 dc, dc2inc) 6 times (30 sts).

Round 6: (2 dc, dc2inc, 2 dc) 6 times (36 sts).

Round 7: (5 dc, dc2inc) 6 times (42 sts).

Rounds 8-13: Dc in each st around.

Round 14: 15 dc, 1 ch, skip 1 dc, 10 dc, 1 ch, skip 1 dc, 15 dc.

Note: the chain spaces in round 14 are where you place the safety eyes later.

Rounds 15-16: Dc in each st around.

Round 17: (5 dc, dc2tog) 6 times (36 sts).

Rounds 18-19: Dc in each st around.

Add the safety eyes in the chain spaces on round 14.

Round 20: (2 dc, dc2tog, 2 dc) 6 times (30 sts).

Round 21: Dc in each st around.

Round 22: (3 dc, dc2tog) 6 times (24 sts).

Round 23: (Dc, dc2tog, dc) 6 times (18 sts).

Round 24: (Dc, dc2tog) 6 times (12 sts).

Round 25: (Dc, dc2tog) 4 times (8 sts).

Fasten off and weave the yarn under each of the FLO, pull tight and hide the end inside the head.

This will be the end of this colour. Trim any yarn left on the cake and set aside. You will continue the next part with the next colour.

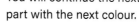

EARS (MAKE 2)

With the next cake yarn colour, work all the stitches in a round.
Do not stuff.

Round 1: Make a MC with 6 dc (6 sts).

Round 2: (Dc2inc) 6 times (12 sts).

Rounds 3–4: Dc in each st around.

Round 5: (Dc, dc2inc) 6 times (18 sts).

Rounds 6–7: Dc in each st around.

Round 8: (Dc, dc2inc, dc) 6 times (24 sts).

Rounds 9–10: Dc in each st around.

Round 11: (Dc, dc2tog, dc) 6 times (18 sts).

Round 12: Dc in each st around.

Round 13: (Dc, dc2tog) 6 times (12 sts).

Pinch the ear closed, dc through both sides with 6 dc and close the opening (6 sts). Now, fold the bottom of the ear in half and dc across once more (3 sts). Fasten off and leave a long tail for attaching.

HAIR

Continuing the current cake yarn colour, work all the stitches in a round.

Round 1: Make a MC with 6 LP dc (6 sts).

Round 2: (LP dc2inc) 6 times (12 sts).

Fasten off and leave a long tail for attaching.

EYELIDS (MAKE 2)

Continuing the current cake yarn colour, work all the stitches in a row. When crocheting in a chain, after turning, dc in the 2nd chain from the hook.

Row 1: Ch 7, turn.

Row 2: 6 dc (6 sts).

Fasten off and leave a long tail for attaching.

MAKING UP

EYES

Outline the safety eyes inserted on round 14 of the head using the small embroidery needle and white and black crochet thread (see page 24).

MUZZLE AND NOSE

Pin the muzzle between the eyes at rounds 14 and 7 with 1–2 stitches before the safety eyes. Place the 3 double crochets at the corners of the muzzle. The muzzle should now be an oval shape, not a round shape. Once the placement is correct, with the large embroidery needle use whip stitches to attach and stuff the muzzle before closing the stitches. Place 6 pins to mark a heart-shaped nose on the muzzle. The 2 top pins marked at round 5 are evenly spaced with 5 stitches between. The outside of the heart will be on round 5, 1 stitch away from the top pins. The bottom pin is in the magic circle at the centre of the muzzle and the inside top pin 3 rounds above the bottom pin. Using the small embroidery needle and the black crochet thread, push your needle through the bottom of the muzzle, and pull it out from the bottom pin of the heart. Embroider a line to each of your pin markings. This will ensure the nose keeps its shape. From there, embroider the heart in a fan-like shape working from one side to the other filling in the spaces between each threaded line. Once finished, outline the heart to complete the look.

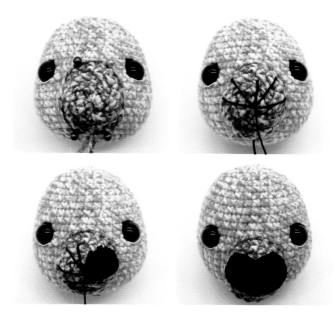

EYELIDS

Use the large embroidery needle to whip stitch the eyelids above each safety eye at an angle with the wrong side showing. On rounds 17–18, 1–2 rounds above the safety eyes, whip stitch the inside corner of the eyelids to the face. Attach the rest of the eyelid at a downward angle across the top of the safety eye. The bottom of the eyelid should end at round 13. When finished, weave in the end.

EARS

Pin the ears to the side of the head between rounds 18 and 19. They should be slightly towards the back of the head, with about 8 stitches between them at the back of the head. Both ears should be facing outwards. When they look even, whip stitch them along the bottom of the ear with the large embroidery needle. Add a few whip stitches near the back of the ear to hold the ears upright and in that position. When finished, weave in the end.

HAIR

The hair will be attached at round 24 of the top of the head, matching up the 12 stitches of the hair with the 12 stitches of round 24. Once centred, use the large embroidery needle and long tail to attach the hair with whip stitches. When finished, weave in the end.

LEGS

Like all other parts, the legs should be pinned to get the correct placement before sewing. The back legs should be at rounds 6–13 and on the sides of the body. Make sure the alpaca can sit on his own before sewing. If not, adjust the legs up or down for 1 or 2 rounds to get a perfect sitting position. Once even, use the large embroidery needle to attach the legs to the body with whip stitches. Add a few whip stitches along the bottom of the legs to ensure they are secured and don't move around. When complete, secure and weave in the end.

Pin the front legs 8 rounds down from the head between rounds 23–24 and on the side of the body. Angle them slightly down with the BLO of the hooves touching the flat surface it is on. If the alpaca is still sitting, start attaching the pieces with whip stitches using the large embroidery needle. If not, adjust the front legs up or down to ensure a good sitting position. Once sewn, add a few extra whip stitches to the bottom of the back of the arms to ensure the arms stay secured and in that position. When complete, secure and weave in the end.

HEAD AND BODY

Before attaching the head to the body, use pins to ensure the placement is correct. Centre the head, matching up the last round of 18 stitches on the body and 18 stitches on the head at round 3. Once you are happy with the placement, attach the head and body by using the large embroidery needle and the long tail left over from the body to whip stitch the two parts together. When finished, weave in the end.

Garrick the Dragon

Garrick the Dragon has been practising his roar. He wants it to be as powerful and fierce as his papa's. Every day, Garrick perches himself to the side of the rocky cliff, and with a big deep breath, he roars down into the canyon. 'Oh, to be as big as Papa,' he thinks. One day, little dragon; one day.

Skill Level

Finished size

9in (22.5cm)

Supplies and materials

Lion Brand Mandala Ombré, 100% acrylic (344yd/315m per 150g)

1 ball in Balance

Size 10 crochet thread in black and white

2.75mm (US C/2) crochet hook

2 x ½in (12mm) safety eyes

Polyester fibre filling

Large and small embroidery needles

Scissors

Sewing pins

Stitch markers

The dragon is made by choosing the colours for specific pieces of the design from either the yarn cake's centre pull or from the outside starting pull. The first colour will be used for the feet, paws and horns, working the ombré for the body and finally the spots in another colour.

Starting with either the inside or the outside of the yarn cake, work all the stitches in a round unless otherwise instructed.

FEET (make 2)

Round 1: Make a MC with 6 dc (6 sts).
Round 2: (Dc2inc) 6 times (12 sts).
Round 3: (Dc, dc2inc) 6 times (18 sts).
Round 4: (Dc, dc2inc, dc) 6 times (24 sts).
Round 5: 7 dc, (BOB, 2 dc) 3 times, BOB, 7 dc (24 sts).
Leaving the last stitch unfinished, cut the yarn and set it aside for a colour change later.

PAWS (make 2)

Continuing the current cake yarn colour, work all the stitches in a round.
Round 1: Make a MC with 6 dc (6 sts).
Round 2: (Dc2inc) 6 times (12 sts).
Round 3: (Dc, dc2inc) 6 times (18 sts).
Round 4: 4 dc, (BOB, 2 dc) 3 times, BOB, 4 dc (18 sts).
Leaving the last stitch unfinished, cut the yarn and set it aside for a colour change later.

HORNS 1 (make 2)

Continuing the current cake yarn colour, work all the stitches in a round from bottom to top.
Do not stuff.
Round 1: Make a MC with 8 dc (8 sts).
Do not pull the string to the magic circle tight; leave a small hole to push the extra yarn end inside.
Round 2: Dc in BLO in each st around (8 sts).
Round 3: 4 dc, (dc2tog) twice (6 sts).
Round 4: Dc in each st around.
Round 5: (Dc, dc2tog) twice (4 sts).
Fasten off and weave the yarn under each of the FLO, pull tight and hide the end inside the horn.
Later, you will connect a new yarn colour to the BLO on round 2 of the horns and continue crocheting, working all the stitches in a round.
This will be the end of this colour. Cut any yarn left on the cake that needs to be trimmed and set aside.
You will continue the next part with the next colour.

TAIL

Continuing the next cake yarn colour, work all the stitches in a round.
Stuff as you crochet.
Round 1: Make a MC with 4 dc (4 sts).
Round 2: (Dc, dc2inc) twice (6 sts).
Round 3: Dc in each st around.
Round 4: 2 dc, (dc2inc) twice, 2 dc (8 sts).
Rounds 5–6: Dc in each st around.

Round 7: 3 dc, (dc2inc) twice, 3 dc (10 sts).
Rounds 8–10: Dc in each st around.
Round 11: 4 dc, (dc2inc) twice, 4 dc (12 sts).
Rounds 12–14: Dc in each st around.
Round 15: 5 dc (dc2inc) twice, 5 dc (14 sts).
Rounds 16–18: Dc in each st around.
Round 19: 6 dc, (dc2inc) twice, 6 dc (16 sts).
Rounds 20–25: Dc in each st around.
Round 26: 7 dc, (dc2inc) twice, 7 dc (18 sts).
Rounds 27–31: Dc in each st around.
Fasten off and leave a long tail for attaching.

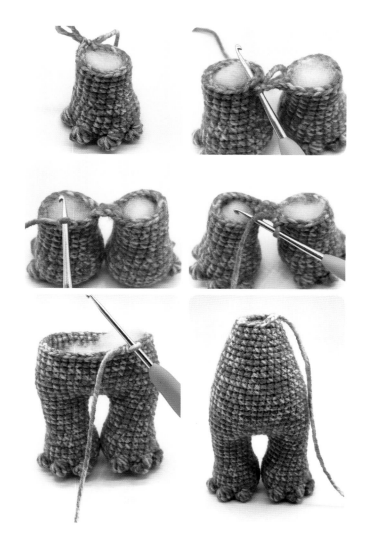

. . . .

BODY

With the next cake yarn colour, work all the stitches
in a round from bottom to top.
Make 2 legs, then connect the legs at round 16
to continue the body. Connect the next yarn colour to
the last stitch of the feet and continue crocheting.
Stuff as you crochet.
Rounds 6–9: Dc in each st around.
Round 10: (Dc, dc2tog, dc) 6 times (18 sts).
Rounds 11–15: Dc in each st around.
For the first leg ONLY, dc 4 extra sts. Fasten off.
Round 16: Ch 3, join the first leg with a dc.
Pay attention to where you join the legs. Join the first leg
in the st after the extra 4 dc. The two feet will now be
positioned with the toes pointed outwards.
Continue around the first leg with 18 dc. 3 dc along the
3 ch, then 18 dc around leg 2 (42 sts).
Place a marker here to remember that the starting
point will be from the beginning of the connecting ch.
Continuing on the front side of ch 3.
Round 17: (3 dc, dc2inc, 3 dc) 6 times (48 sts).
Rounds 18–21: Dc in each st around.
Round 22: (3 dc, dc2tog, 3 dc) 6 times (42 sts).
Rounds 23–26: Dc in each st around.
Round 27: (5 dc, dc2tog) 6 times (36 sts).
Rounds 28–30: Dc in each st around.

Round 31: (2 dc, dc2tog, 2 dc) 6 times (30 sts).
Rounds 32–34: Dc in each st around.
Round 35: (3 dc, dc2tog) 6 times (24 sts).
Rounds 36–37: Dc in each st around.
Round 38: (Dc, dc2tog, dc) 6 times (18 sts).
Round 39: Dc in each st around.
Round 40: (Dc, dc2tog) 6 times (12 sts).
Fasten off and leave a long tail for attaching.

ARMS (MAKE 2)

Connect the continuing yarn colour to the last stitch of the paws and continue crocheting, working all the stitches in a round. Stuff as you crochet up to round 15.

Rounds 5–9: Dc in each st around.

Round 10: (Dc, dc2tog) 6 times (12 sts).

Rounds 11–24: Dc in each st around.

Pinch the leg closed. If your seam is not centred with the bobble stitches on the paws, add or subtract 1–3 stitches. Dc through both sides with 6 dc and close the opening (6 sts).

Fasten off and leave a long tail for attaching.

HEAD

Continuing the current cake yarn colour, work all the stitches in a round from bottom to top. Stuff as you crochet.

Round 1: Make a MC with 6 dc (6 sts).

Round 2: (Dc2inc) 6 times (12 sts).

Round 3: (Dc, dc2inc) 6 times (18 sts).

Round 4: (Dc, dc2inc, dc) 6 times (24 sts).

Round 5: (3 dc, dc2inc) 6 times (30 sts).

Round 6: (2 dc, dc2inc, 2 dc) 6 times (36 sts).

Round 7: (5 dc, dc2inc) 6 times (42 sts).

Rounds 8–12: Dc in each st around.

Round 13: 15 dc, 1 ch, skip 1 dc, 10 dc, 1 ch, skip 1 dc, 15 dc (42 sts).

Note: the chain spaces in round 13 are where you place the safety eyes later.

Rounds 14–16: Dc in each st around.

Round 17: (5 dc, dc2tog) 6 times (36 sts).

Add the safety eyes in the chain spaces on round 13.

Rounds 18–19: Dc in each st around.

Round 20: (2 dc, dc2tog, 2 dc) 6 times (30 sts).

Round 21: Dc in each st around.

Round 22: (3 dc, dc2tog) 6 times (24 sts).

Round 23: (Dc, dc2tog, dc) 6 times (18 sts).

Round 24: (Dc, dc2tog) 6 times (12 sts).

Round 25: (Dc, dc2tog) 4 times (8 sts).

Fasten off and weave the yarn under each of the FLO, pull tight and hide the end inside the head.

HORNS 2 (MAKE 2)

Hold the horn upside down and connect the current yarn colour to the BLO on round 2 of the horns. Continue crocheting, working all the stitches in a round.

Round 6: (FLO dc2inc) 8 times (16 sts).

Fasten off and leave a long tail for attaching.

EARS (MAKE 2)

Continuing the current cake yarn colour, work all the stitches in a round. Do not stuff.

Round 1: Make a MC with 4 dc (4 sts).

Round 2: (Dc, dc2inc) twice (6 sts).

Round 3: (Dc2inc) 6 times (12 sts).

Rounds 4–5: Dc in each st around.

Round 6: (Dc, dc2inc) 6 times (18 sts).

Rounds 7–9: Dc in each st around.

Round 10: 14 dc, (dc2tog) twice (16 sts).

Round 11: 12 dc, (dc2tog) twice (14 sts).
Round 12: (5 dc, dc2tog) twice (12 sts).
Round 13: 8 dc, (dc2tog) twice (10 sts).
Round 14: Dc in each st around.
Round 15: 2 dc only, leaving the rest of the stitches unworked.
Pinch the ear closed, dc through both sides with 5 dc and close the opening (5 sts).
Fasten off and leave a long tail for attaching.

WINGS (MAKE 2)

Continuing the current cake yarn colour, work all the stitches in a row.
When crocheting in a chain, after turning, dc in the 2nd chain from the hook.
Row 1: With a long starting tail, ch 6, turn.
Row 2: 2 dc, 3 dc in the next st, 2 dc, ch, turn (7 sts).
Row 3: 3 dc, 3 dc in the next st, 3 dc, ch, turn (9 sts).
Row 4: 4 dc, 3 dc in the next st, 4 dc, ch turn (11 sts).
Row 5: 5 dc, (dc, ch, sl st in the 3rd loop of the ch, dc) in next st, 5 dc (14 sts).
Fasten off and leave long tails for attaching.

MAKING UP

EYES

Outline the safety eyes inserted on round 13 of the head using the small embroidery needle and white and black crochet thread (see page 24).

HORNS

Pin the horns 5 rounds above the safety eyes, starting at round 19. Leave 4 stitches between them and place them slightly forward from the centre of the head. Make sure to have the horns pointing upwards and to the centre of the top of the head. Then attach the horns by seam stitching around the detailed edge with the large embroidery needle. To make the first stitch, slip the needle under a stitch on the head, then bring the needle up through the first stitch on the horn edge and down through the next stitch. This creates the detail of a stitched seam on the horn edge. Repeat these steps around the horn. Once both horns are complete, weave in and hide the leftover tail inside the head.

EARS

Pin the ears to the side of the head between rounds 19 and 20 below the horns, 2–3 stitches from the safety eyes, with the inner cup of the ear toward the head. Once the placement is correct, whip stitch the ears in place with the large embroidery needle. Weave in the end when finished.

ARMS

The arms should be pinned 1–2 rounds down from the head between rounds 38 and 39 and on the sides of the body. Leave at least 6–7 stitches between them on the back, and angle them slightly towards the front of the body. If they are even, you can start whip stitching the pieces to the body with the large embroidery needle. If not, adjust the arms up or down to ensure a good placement. Add a few whip stitches to the back portion of the arms to secure the correct positioning, and weave in the end.

HEAD AND BODY

Before attaching the head to the body, use pins to ensure the placement is correct. You want the head to be slightly forward to create the look of a larger chin. Once aligned, attach the head and body by using the large embroidery needle and the long tail left over from the body to whip stitch the two parts together. Weave in the end when finished.

WINGS

The wings are placed in the middle of the back 6 rounds down from the head starting between rounds 35 and 36. The tips point upwards with 1 stitch between them and the last row of the wings facing out. Using the large embroidery needle, attach the turning edge of the wings to the centre of the back with whip stitches. When complete, secure and weave in the end.

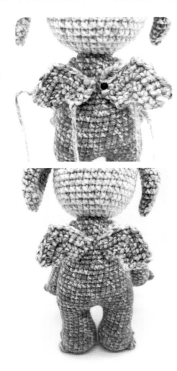

SPOTS

Mark clusters of spots on the head, body, arm, foot and back with pins. Then, using the next yarn colour or scrap yarn, push the large embroidery needle through the body and exit a few stitches from where you want the spots. Tie a knot at the bottom of the yarn where it exits the body. Insert the embroidery needle 1 stitch over from the knot. Repeat this for at least 3–10 more spots depending on how and where you want the spots. Pull the embroidery needle through the body and out where it entered, then tie off and hide the ends inside the body. Repeat in many locations around the body and face. You could also use two or three different colours for the spots.

TAIL

Attach the tail to the lower back between rounds 19 and 24 and centred between the back legs. Position the tail where the dragon stands. Using the large embroidery needle, sew it on with whip stitches once the placement is correct. When complete, secure and weave in the end.

ABOUT THE AUTHOR

Jacki Donhou is a native of Las Vegas, Nevada, who learned to crochet after moving to Washington state and becoming a stay-at-home mom. After a few years of following other people's designs, she decided to try creating her own, inspired by her love of animals, and her memories of her kids and how they loved their favourite toys when they were growing up. Since then, she has developed a loyal social media following as people have fallen in love with her unique and fun amigurumi designs. Fuelled by coffee, giggles and a strange addiction to colourful yarn, Jacki is always looking for new ways to make people smile.

ACKNOWLEDGEMENTS

What a fabulous journey this step in my life has been. The support everyone has given me is truly amazing.

To my amazing publisher Jonathan Bailey, thank you for taking a chance on me. To the great team at GMC Publications: Tom, Jude, Nicola and Jane R for patiently editing all my text; and Robin, Jane L, Andrew, Martin, Cathy and Alex for all their hard work beautifully designing, illustrating and photographing my book and keeping my vision.

I was extremely lucky to work with the most fabulous group of pattern testers: Tommy Adams, Sarah Wright, Christina Krieger, Simone Mitchell, Jessica Öhrt, Sarah Prather, Lenny Handoko and Yetty Sadikin. My patterns couldn't have come to life without all your time and dedication to this long process.

To the wonderful people at Lion Brand Yarns, thank you for the beautiful Mandala Ombré yarn cakes for my designs and for supporting this book of mine.

To my dearest friends that helped me to the finish line: Michelle, Joni, Sonja, Jo and Christina, thank you for the continual push and encouragement over the years.

But most of all, to my amazing little family. My best friend and husband Chris in "logistics" for constantly being there for me when I had ups and downs, helping me iron out the ideas I had problems putting down on paper, and for your support from day one. To Athena, Roger and Charlotte, you three will always be my lifelong inspiration! My parents and siblings for being my noteworthy cheerleaders year after year. I love you all forever!

INDEX

INDEX

First published 2023 by
Guild of Master Craftsman Publications Ltd
Castle Place, 166 High Street, Lewes,
East Sussex BN7 1XU

Text © Jacki Donhou, 2023
Copyright in the Work © GMC Publications Ltd, 2023

ISBN 978-1-78494-667-8

A catalogue record for this book is available
from the British Library.

Publisher Jonathan Bailey
Production Director Jim Bulley
Senior Project Editor Tom Kitch
Editor Nicola Hodgson
Design Manager Robin Shields
Design JC Lanaway
Photography Andrew Perris
New Illustrations Martin Woodward

Colour origination by GMC Reprographics

Printed and bound in China

TO ORDER A BOOK, CONTACT:

GMC Publications Ltd, Castle Place,
166 High Street, Lewes, East Sussex,
BN7 1XU, United Kingdom
Tel: +44 (0)1273 488005
www.gmcbooks.com